INSTIGATOR!

INSTIGATOR!

CREATING CHANGE
WITHOUT BEING
THE LOUDEST VOICE
IN THE ROOM

LYSNE TAIT

MANUSCRIPTS
PRESS

INSTIGATOR!
Creating Change without Being the Loudest Voice in the Room

ISBN   979-8-88926-140-7 *Paperback*

979-8-88926-141-4 *Hardcover*

979-8-88926-139-1 *Ebook*

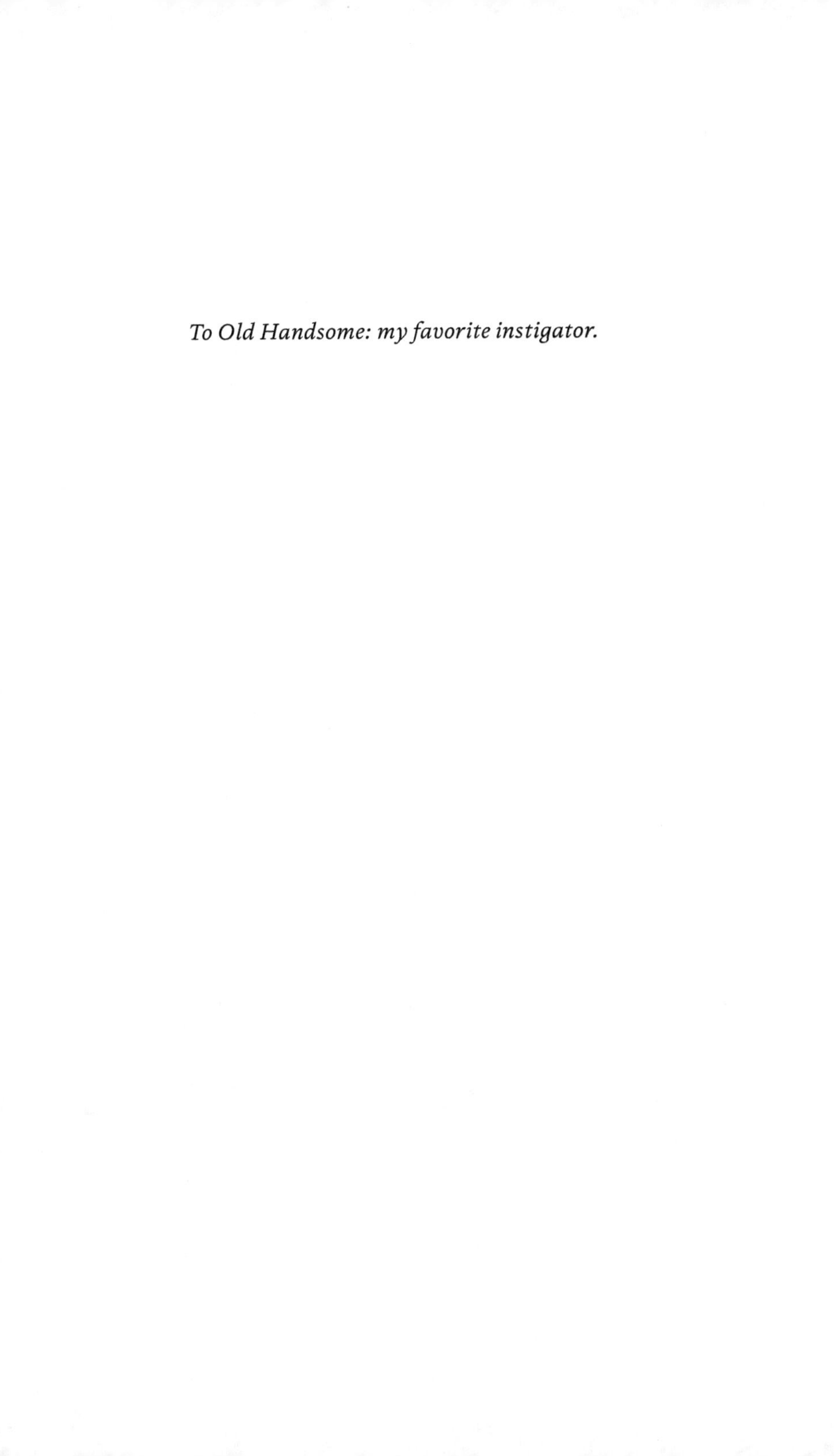

To Old Handsome: my favorite instigator.

CONTENTS

INTRODUCTION

I woke up feeling oppositional. The morning drive didn't help. I think we were a week away from a full moon. Cars were turning left from the right lane. A concrete truck decided at the last minute they weren't turning and skewed back into my lane. The lights were unpredictable. I had a meeting scheduled with my editor that I wanted so much to cancel, but I didn't. I took a deep breath and reset my expectations. Being able to reframe the conversation—looking at what is in the way and finding out how to look at it differently—is part of being an instigator. The solution will be richer if I can use a different lens to solve the problem or come at it from another angle, even if the conversation is just with myself.

While doing research for this book and looking up synonyms for instigator and disruptor, I found myself stuck. The words they both have in common are firebrand, ringleader, and rabble-rouser. So many terms have negative connotations. Initially, I worried about this, but I realized they have negative connotations because people don't care for change. And even those who ask for change aren't always ready when it comes. Instigators know change has to happen. They know things will be uncomfortable for a while and prepare for that, because change won't happen if most people are happy or at least comfortable.

Then, with the gift of ADHD, I started listening to podcasts touting instigators, but they weren't what I was thinking about at all. The first podcast, called *Instigator*, is all about a woman who is the first person of color (POC) woman president in her business. While that is laudable, I saw a difference between being an *instigator* and being the *inaugural person in a role*. The first does not mean you changed popular thinking, although it may change the thinking of those around or behind you. Instigation, to me, involves doing something different—bucking the established system. The next podcast just talked about people who started fights in sports. That's not what I'm talking about either—too negative and loud.

To create change there must be some discomfort, or else we wouldn't want to change. A good part of my discomfort arose from my frustration and oppositional feelings—in short, feeling my inertia would win if I remained comfortable. I went to my meeting and told my editor I didn't want to be there and why. We talked through a few things, and here I am—actually writing. It was helpful to talk about why I didn't want to write. Some of the things I said were excuses, and others were reasons. But I came to the realization that the process of writing takes many forms, and just putting words down is only one. Reading, talking, complaining, and listening to media about my subject all lead to what I put down on the page. My voice is important. I do have something to say about instigators who might make the ideas of leadership more accessible to some. It's fine that others are also writing about leadership. It's a huge subject, and there are as many ways to lead as there are leaders.

I think of instigators as slightly irritating—like the dust that creates pearls in oysters or a mosquito in a tent. What was that African proverb? "If you think you are too small to make a difference, you haven't spent the night with a mosquito." Instigators do not have to be the loudest ones in the room. Quiet leadership is redirecting the conversation and having awareness of the power dynamics in the room—a whisper here, a suggestion there. Instigation is both tactical *and* strategic. It sees the details and big picture, providing both the map and the compass. It is not necessarily impulsive. It takes patience and awareness to be a successful instigator.

For far too long, the western style of leadership has been to take charge, fake it until they make it, and mete out rewards and punishments to manipulate followers, employees, children, or coworkers to make the leader look good.

This book is different. It is a book for instigators who want to make the world a better place, regardless of who gets the credit.

I am writing this book for those who don't necessarily read leadership or social activism books. I want people who read this to feel empowered to instigate change in their lives. Small changes help the big picture too. Networking events create connections that can help move the needle. Pulling people together is one of the main traits of the instigator. I don't want this book to be blatantly about social activism and politics. Instead, I want the every-day average person to feel comfortable thinking about themselves as an instigator.

I want them to read the stories about other, regular people who did things a little differently and contributed to the lifting of our society. I want to give them steps (pay attention, get your ego out of the way, connect with others) so they, too, can choose to do things differently.

My version of the instigator is quiet, determined, and behind the scenes. Instigators don't have to be loud. In fact, quiet persistence makes it harder to ignore the message. After all, we have flashing lights and moving ads in our faces every day while our devices show commercials constantly telling us what to do or what we are doing wrong. And then we have our internal editors scolding us at every turn. There is too much noise in the world.

Change doesn't have to be on a large scale. It can take place in small increments. That's why instigators are important. They jiggle the structure just a little, shaking away the extraneous bits so we can see the problem.

You don't need a bunch of credentials or qualifications to be an instigator—just a healthy dose of empathy, courage, and awareness. Over the years, I have helped start a school. I founded a period-poverty prevention nonprofit called Helping Women Period. I also created five Facebook networking groups for women. I am fascinated with creating connections for jobs, volunteers, and other needs.

When I helped start the school, I was a year out of college. They hired me the day before school opened, and I walked into a situation with no tables, no curriculum, and really no experience other than half a year of student teaching and half a year of subbing. The nonprofit was an accident. It was supposed to be a one-and-done event and ended up being so much bigger. My degree was in teaching English. I had no experience with inventory, supply chain management, marketing, or even spreadsheets. The networking group grew out of a need to connect with others in a way that differed from traditional networking. I will go into more detail about all of these experiences later in this book.

So we can all start on the same page, here are some traits of the instigator:

Instigators are aware. They listen and pay attention to others in the group—not only to the words but also to body language. Who crosses their arms when the subject of change comes up? Who is dealing with heavy situations at home: a new baby, an illness, or other stressors? Who wants the last word every time? What needs are they missing?

Instigators ask questions. What if? What would it look like if we did that? What is our ultimate goal? How do we get there? And then they wait, giving others the time to really think about the questions, goals, or process.

Uncomfortable silences help cause the friction that creates change.

Calmness and *an investment in free discourse* are hallmarks of an instigator. Knowing what the end goal is and not taking disagreements with an idea as dislikes of the individual are also hallmarks. I think this is one of the hardest parts—learning not to take criticism personally. I am pretty calm by nature, but I'm also a people-pleaser, and it took me years to figure out how to look at the merits of an idea without giving an emotional reaction.

Instigators look at a problem and find *nontraditional solutions.* My father actually figures out three ways to solve a problem before he starts working on it. Most issues instigators solve are ones for which traditional methods exacerbated the problem or at least didn't solve it.

Finally, instigators are *quiet, calm,* and *insistent.* They are busy listening to others and considering possibilities and solutions. They don't need to be the center of attention because they are confident in themselves and committed to fomenting change. Purpose drives them with the desire to make things better instead of the desire for praise or fame.

There are ways to create change without bullying your way to the top. The loudest voice need not win. By listening, being aware, and asking questions, the quiet voice can get things done without drama and fanfare. Learning this skill, this ability to influence change, to redirect a group from the inside without posturing or performative actions, is true leadership. The instigator leader is stronger because they are doing the work, not just directing it.

The traditional way is not sustainable—if only because there is too much information at everyone's fingertips. Leadership can no longer be top-down, and no one can hold all the cards anymore. Those of us in the back need to step up and institute lasting change for all because we know what the needs are, and we aren't necessarily interested in personal gain. Motivation for change must be organic and come from within the group and individuals. We must disrupt the system.

Redirecting the conversation and awareness of the power dynamics in the room—a whisper here, a suggestion there—are hallmarks of quiet leadership. Instigation is both tactical *and* strategic. It sees the details and the big picture, providing both the fuel and the compass. It is not necessarily impulsive. It takes patience and awareness to be a successful instigator.

This book is for those in the back who have ideas but don't know how to put them forward, who see a need and want to fill it because it is the right thing to do, and who know what needs to be done. Sometimes, being loud about the change that needs to happen is dangerous and only provides temporary relief. Quiet, inclusive leadership gets more people to buy in, which leads to longer-lasting change.

If that is something you want to learn more about, keep reading!

PART 1

A rising tide lifts all boats.

—JOHN F. KENNEDY

ADDRESSING THE GAP

The first time I met Kristi Hemmer in person, I had just opened my front door. She was standing on my doorstep, a small backpack on her arm, ready to spend a week with me. Her blue eyes were sparkling, and she was just so positive, energetic, and full of life. I felt as if we had been friends forever.

We had met online about two years before but had only really spoken on the phone a few times. Years ago, Kristi taught at the Jakarta International School in Jakarta, Indonesia, with my aunt and uncle, and she reached out to me because she heard about my nonprofit, Helping Women Period. She was working on a book, *Quit Being So Good: Stories of an Unapologetic Woman*, and wanted to ask me about my experiences with expectations, especially in light of the work I was doing in the menstrual equity space. Part of her book discussed looking for the *helpers*, and Kristi wanted the perspective of someone who was a helper.

Now, she was staying with me as part of her book tour. One of my favorite things to do is to connect people, so I helped her arrange a few readings and scheduled some workshops. We even did one together! I had never been interested in self-help books until I read hers. It was compelling, had short chapters, and the messages resonated with me. I think the fact she had been an educator helped. The information was clear, and the stories were engaging. I love reading about real people. Kristi's book was refreshingly open, honest, and real.

We held the workshop we taught together in a small, independent bookstore on a sunny spring evening. I was nervous, because this was my first time teaching a workshop, and I wasn't sure how it would go. Who would be there? Would they *really* be interested in learning about alternative menstrual products? How exactly were we going to combine my workshop with Kristi's book?

We chose to talk about the three steps in her book that some might say dismantled patriarchy: 1) Take up space, 2) be first, and 3) look for the helpers (Hemmer 2021, 14). I could talk a bit about being a helper, explain how Helping Women Period worked, and introduce some alternative menstrual products. The group engaged themselves into the discussion and asked insightful questions. The evening was delightful, even if we only had seven participants.

After Kristi continued her book tour, a few friends who attended one of the readings decided to start a book club. I joined because I liked those women and thought I could learn from them. At first, I was hesitant, because I really didn't care for nonfiction books, but I decided to give it a go. Besides, the first book we read was Kristi's. Talking about the different chapters and looking at the three steps in view of our own worlds was fun. We had a great conversation about how to take up space and were able to vocalize our discomfort at just *thinking* about taking up space. I'd never had that kind of discussion before, and I was looking forward to the next meeting.

The second book we read was Glennon Doyle's *Untamed*. Everyone else in the group loved it, but I was angry. I wanted to improve my life, but I didn't want to leave my husband! Her book starts with her change in marital status and how she "remembered her wild," meaning she found her true self after falling in love with a woman (Doyle 2020, 5). I wondered: Was there a way to make change without doing drastic things? I am happy it worked for Glennon, but I felt left out because I didn't want big things. I wanted a way to find change in the little things in my everyday life.

The third book we read was *Year of Yes: How to Dance It Out, Stand in the Sun and Be Your Own Person* by Shonda Rhimes. I was willing to give it a chance because it sounded like a good theory, but the last book we read still disappointed me. I did not know who Shonda was. I wasn't familiar with the TV shows she wrote, such as *Grey's Anatomy* and *Bridgerton*. However, the other women in the group were fans of *Grey's Anatomy* and felt excited about reading the book. Shonda has many resources at her disposal, so saying yes to everything for one year didn't cause any concern about her career, her financial status, or her family life. It felt like the entire book was more of a humble brag than a real way to move forward. I didn't have half the resources she had. I had to watch my kids and make the dinner. I wasn't in a position to say yes to opportunities on the scale that she did. I am a regular person. I didn't have a publicist and wouldn't have the opportunity to say yes to an interview with Jimmy Kimmel (Rimes 2015, 36–45).

I am not saying there isn't anything to learn from these books. They have some great messages. The writing is good, and I am sure they spent a lot of time on their books. However, the catalyst for the change they describe instigates from the outside. Would they have created change in their lives without the divorce, without the comfort or privilege of wealth? Would the change they discussed be as successful? I am not convinced.

The problem with most self-help or thought-leader books is that most of them hinge on a *huge* life-changing event or the authors have the means to do things no matter the cost. We don't need to make such sweeping changes. It is totally okay to make incremental ones, which is, in part, why I wrote this book.

Anyone can help motivate change. For most people, it all starts with baby steps. Baby steps are not mincing little footfalls, Have you ever watched a baby learn to walk? There is a lot of falling down and lurching across the room—one big, shaky step, followed by two little rebalancing steps. No infant just starts walking across the room. If you want to create change, you have to give yourself grace for those falls and stumbles and focus on the individual footsteps. You will make it across the room, maybe not on the first or second attempt. But you will learn and adjust, so later you can go across with ease.

Books like James Clear's *Atomic Habits* focus on the little steps, the small actions with which you can make an incremental change in your life (Clear 2018, 28). But there are far more books where change comes from a break caused by an abnormal event.

Big changes are great. They make good headlines, sell books, and get media attention. I can't even count the number of social media ads that show up in my feed touting magical solutions that will help lose massive amounts of weight without exercise or eliminate all wrinkles with one product. No magic wand or simple solution exists to make huge changes. For those big changes to happen, we need to start with the little changes like better food choices, drinking more water, using moisturizers, and paying attention.

It is so easy to look at the big things in our world that need to change—wars, poverty, homelessness, apathy— and become depressed. Bad news bombards us daily, if not hourly, and decisions made by people in power affect many but benefit few. War in the Middle East has been a refrain since before I was born. People hold up cardboard signs asking for help, food, or money on street corners all over the US. Facebook, Instagram, and X (formerly known as Twitter) have people spouting about how other generations are horrid, lazy, and unmotivated. It is overwhelming. We can choose to let the helplessness swallow us, or we can do something. Looking for the good and the beauty in every day helps. We need to do what we can. Even the littlest action can create ripples that move across the world.

Before jumping into becoming an instigator, it might help to examine some traditional beliefs that are sometimes hard to let go of. First, the important thing is the process, *not* the end result. If you are here looking for fame and fortune, you might as well turn around. True instigators detach themselves from the outcome. They have no concern about who gets the credit. Rather, they want equity.

Second, any action will create more questions. Remember those ripples that go outward from the dropped pebbles? If you watch closely, ripples will echo back to the spot where that action first occurred. You must pay attention to that feedback. This is the time to ask questions, and it is also the time to sit back and listen. Let things be uncomfortable. Be patient. If there is no discomfort, there will be no change.

CHAPTER 2

POWER AND INSTIGATORS

Instigation is using your authentic power to create change. When we use our own power to change things rather than control people, we are living the life of the instigator. Power is a word fraught with baggage, especially if you are a woman or identify as one. Literature promoted the idea of power and control together even before Sun Tzu and his book on war.

We have had enough of that relationship. It is time to teach a new kind of quiet power of connection, awareness, and empathy. We must relinquish fear and the desire for control. We must practice the Buddhist idea of non-attachment: letting go of the desired outcome while believing what we are doing is the correct course of action (Vredeveld 2024). When we see something that needs change, we can nudge others to move in the right direction. But when we start pushing and controlling things and looking for acknowledgment, we fall back into the traditional ways of dictatorial leadership.

Finding our own power is work. Slipping into the old ways because they are familiar is easy. After all, others have filled our lives with stories about how it is important to have power over others. Those are the people with the most status in our current society. Our schools were based on the idea of a leader giving orders, a hold-over from the two World Wars and our patriarchal society. Letting go of the idea of status, of the idea of control, is scary but necessary. We cannot keep doing what we have always done and expect different results.

I'm reading a book called *The Power Code: More Joy. Less Ego. Maximum Impact for Women (and Everyone)* by Katty Kay and Claire Shipman. It is an interesting look at two different kinds of power. One is more traditional and generally associated with men, and another is more innovative and generally associated with women. The first is the power over things (people, animals, stocks, and bonds). It is authoritarian, forcing people to do things in a top-down manner. The other, nontraditional form of power attributed mostly to women is the power to *do* things and create change. This power structure is more like that of the instigator—creating change to better the community, not just to better the one in power (Kay and Shipman 2023, 24–30).

The power to do is inclusive, looking at the community as a whole and acknowledging that work and home life are inseparable. Change created with this kind of power, instigator power, is longer lasting and more inclusive. The purpose is not to have some kind of ego-driven control over others but to change things in a communal way.

This comprehensive attitude toward power and authority makes a better, stronger community because the people affected have a say.

There is power in quietly starting organizations, championing causes, and creating solutions without demanding credit. There's strength in selflessly figuring out new ways to solve problems, in being persistent, and in remembering people's names and faces. Women often spend time influencing and redirecting others. In fact, many women I know are instigators. Do they consider themselves powerful? I certainly do!

This quote from an interview with the first female editor of the *Economist*, Zanny Minton Beddoes in *The Power Code*, spoke directly to the instigator in me:

> "I think one of the most effective ways to be a leader is to make sure other people take the credit," she says. "Which, by the way, is also hugely motivating."

> "It's not about you, it's about what's best for the organization" (Kay and Shipman 2023, 55).

Instigation doesn't work if you are just looking for applause. The beauty of being an instigator is that your efforts end up creating a bigger wave than if you had just been loud. Instigators are not bullies. They are interested in consensus, inclusion, and solutions.

Many people I know, especially women, shy away from the idea of power. We use self-deprecation as a shield.

I'm reminded of Marianne Williamson's statement in *A Return to Love: Reflections on the Principles of a Course in Miracles*:

> Our deepest fear is not that we are inadequate. Our deepest fear is that we are powerful beyond measure. It is our light, not our darkness that most frightens us. We ask ourselves, "Who am I to be brilliant, gorgeous, talented, fabulous?" Actually, who are you not to be? (Williamson 2007, 190).

I think we need to take a look at what we envision when we talk about power. Do we see Dr. Frankenstein, laughing maniacally, with wild hair and eyes? Or do we see the quiet self-possession of Rosa Parks? Do we want power over things, or do we want the power to do things?

Because you are reading this book, I assume you want to do things, make change, and move the status quo to a more equitable situation. We cannot let the fear of being powerful or the learned behavior of deprecation deter us from taking that first tiny step.

As an eternal optimist, I believe most people are good and want the best for their communities. I still struggle daily with accepting that I am "powerful beyond measure." That self-deprecating bit deeply ingrains itself within. I almost wrote that I struggle with accepting I am *not* inadequate. I was hesitant to write I am powerful. It is a continual learning process.

One way I fight against this imposter syndrome is to work on learning in public. Writing this book and explaining my process, difficulties, and successes is one way. I want to be vulnerable and let you see you aren't alone while also maintaining my expert status.

Traditional western leadership does not agree with me. I can't tell you the number of times I see "fake it until you make it" and "don't ever let them see you sweat" in advice columns. Leaders hide decisions from employees or students while they hold all the cards. This is also what is wrong with education today. We are no longer in factory settings. An authority figure doesn't control the dissemination of information. We have phones, tablets, and computers with access to more information than we know what to do with at our fingertips.

Authority figures need to be collaborative and transparent in decisions. We need to help our students and employees learn how to discern truth from fiction, learn how to find the information they need, and not spoon-feed them only what we think they need to know. Letting others know our weaknesses and internal conflicts or what we care about only helps them be more comfortable with who they are.

I know what you are going to say... For you, it is different. Right? Learning is private. I read, I absorb, and then I regurgitate the information. I don't want anyone to see me fail, get frustrated, or become angry. Why the heck would I want to make my private thoughts and stumbles public? What will I gain from sharing my failures or admitting I don't know all the answers?

First of all, yes. Everyone learns differently, and everyone's process will not be the same, I'll give you that. Even though vulnerability traditionally associates with weakness, I believe it shows true strength.

Officially, learning in public refers to the concept of sharing the *process* of thinking rather than just the end product. I didn't just have this idea and decide to write about it. I had a bud of an idea and needed to push through all the noise to get to the middle.

I'm going to share some of that noise with you. The following is one of my morning pages, a daily exercise I learned from *Drawing on the Right Side of the Brain* by Betty Edwards.

Sometimes, words come forward so quickly I can barely type fast enough. Other times, it's like picking dried glue the kids spilled out of the crevices in the back seat. There's a lump of some kind. I can feel it next to my heart, impeding my breath. I want to kick, punch, or scream. My brain feels sluggish, unwilling to move forward or go around that block. I find myself scrolling through social media, looking for a cozy mystery or a bad romance to read or eighties TV. I contemplate doing the dishes or vacuuming, even though it isn't my turn. That's when I usually realize I'm procrastinating—avoiding that lump and the aching blank page.

The mass later turns into a headache, and I blame the weather. I am unwilling to take responsibility yet for the lack of progress in my writing. It's a big step for me to accept that I am writing. Putting actual words on the page that kind of flow together and transmit ideas across is writing. Some days, it's all I can do to just let my brain churn through the thoughts. That is writing, too, by the way.

Sitting in the coffee shop, I thought a change of atmosphere would help. I can hear the beat of the music through my headphones. I have a half-sweet brown sugar cardamom latte next to me, soothing, anti-tinnitus rushing creek sounds in my headphones, and forty minutes to get words onto the page. I'm ignoring emails and Facebook and the lady next to me with red reading glasses like mine messing with something in her purse.

This place was empty when I first came in, and now it's full. Winter coats and hats have made a reappearance after the seventy-degree weather of the weekend. It's gray and cold outside in the mid-thirties, and it snowed all day yesterday, although it didn't stick. The uncomfortable seats along the window are full, the computers are open, and my reading glasses are dirty, so when I look up the lights split into arcs, and I can't see any faces. Which is probably good—chances are I'd know someone, and we would have to chat. I miss my favorite coffee shop. It was darker and less well-known. I could go into the back and be quiet and type without interruption.

Here is where I start getting stuck, mired in my own insecurity and indecision. I wonder where this book is really going and what I really want to say. I liked the voice in the piece I wrote this morning. I'm worried I don't have enough stories or I have the wrong stories. Will I get on an unhelpful tangent? Are they complete enough with a beginning, middle, end, tension, and description? Do I have a clear enough vision to even start asking questions in an interview? And who would I interview?

Usually, my spiral ends there. I negotiate with myself: go do something else for ten minutes, then come back to write. Often, I go away to read, wash the dishes, or play on my phone, and I don't come back. And then I chastise myself for flaking out about letting everyone, including myself, down.

Being able to reframe the conversation, being aware of what the blockage is, and figuring out how to look at it in a different way is part of being an instigator. If I can use a different lens to solve the problem, or come at it from another angle, the solution will be all the richer for it. By using my morning pages, I can get rid of the noise in my head and start looking at the issue in a different way. How meta! I am using instigator techniques to write the book about being an instigator.

After you read the stories in this book, I want you to walk away with ideas about how you can create change in your own world. I want you to be excited about your power to do things, influence others, and be invested in the process, not necessarily the specific outcome. I hope to show you true leadership is the ability to instigate communal change. The days of figurehead leadership are over.

CHAPTER 3

CREATING A MOVEMENT

Being an instigator means creating from a grassroots perspective. It means identifying an issue, bringing attention to it, and taking steps to rectify it without wedding yourself to the outcome. That's because you want things to change and have an idea of where you would like to go next. However, when you are working with others, you need to allow the outcome to be what it is.

I've been thinking about famous instigators, and they are hard to find. The best instigators are *not* well known because they are creating change from the inside. I can come up with a lot of fictional instigators—Frodo Baggins, Harry Potter, Alanna of Trebond, , and the entire Star Wars series. Many people want to identify with these characters, as they fall into situations where they suddenly need to take charge, but don't have the traditional skills normally required. Yet, surprisingly, they end up saving humanity.

By contrast, real-life instigators don't always save humanity, but they do help it move forward a bit. So much of our forward progress has been due to people addressing the gaps.

Rosa Parks is one of my favorite famous instigators. Her simple act of remaining in her seat on December 1, 1955, created a monumental change in society.

But she wasn't the first Black woman to refuse to move seats on a bus. Other Black women were arrested, including Claudette Colvin, a fifteen-year-old member of the NAACP youth council of which Rosa Parks was an advisor. On March 2, 1955, Colvin was riding the bus home after school when she refused to give up her seat to a white woman. The bus driver stopped and called the police to forcibly remove Claudette from the bus. The police charged her with three offenses: disturbing the peace, violating the segregation laws, and assault and battery of a police officer. Annie Larkins Price, a classmate of Colvin who was also on the bus, said Claudette was yelling about her constitutional rights. However, Annie said she did not see an assault.

After her arrest, the juvenile court convicted Claudette of all three charges. When her lawyer appealed the case to the Montgomery Circuit Court on May 6, 1955, they dropped the first two charges but maintained the conviction for assaulting a police officer. Civil rights leaders, including Martin Luther King Jr., spoke to the police commissioner about her case, and her minister bailed her out. While her actions are not well known, they created a spark in the Montgomery, Alabama, community (Hoose 2009, 31–50).

Along with four other women who refused to give up their seats in 1955 (Aurelia Browder, Susie McDonald, Mary Louise Smith, and Jeanetta Reese), Colvin's experience helped push Rosa Parks into action. History hasn't been kind to Claudette—she was dark-skinned, young, and didn't have *good* hair, so the leaders of the civil rights movement didn't think she would help them keep up appearances, and therefore they did not want to use her as a symbol. Since Rosa knew Claudette through her work with the NAACP Youth Council, she could learn from Claudette's experience and the experiences of the other women. (Hoose 2009, 53–59, 79, 84–88).

In the photos I have seen of her, Rosa Parks seems to have a sweet demeanor and a lovely smile. The story, as I have always heard it, started on December 1, 1955. Rosa was tired after a long day of work and boarded the Montgomery, Alabama, bus. In those days, there was bus segregation. Blacks were in the back, and whites were in the first four rows. Rosa sat just behind the white section. The bus driver had the authority to move the "Whites Only" sign if the first four rows filled up. This evening, he came back and moved the sign one more row and told Rosa and the three other Black people sitting in that row they needed to move toward the back of the bus.

The three others moved, but Rosa just moved over one seat, so she was by the window, and refused to go back. The driver said he would have her arrested, and she told him to go ahead. She wasn't moving. Police arrested and charged her with disorderly conduct and breaking a local ordinance. Her trial, held on December 5, 1955, took thirty minutes. After finding her guilty, they charged her ten dollars plus four dollars in court fees (Theoharis 2013, 65).

Rosa appealed her conviction and formally challenged the racial segregation ordinances in Montgomery. The next day, the Montgomery bus boycott began, spearheaded by the Women's Political Council which had printed off thirty-five thousand handbills asking the Black community to stay off buses. The boycott ran for 381 days until the city repealed the segregation ordinance.

Rosa Parks wasn't tired. She wasn't old. She wasn't just giving up. Ms. Parks had been an activist for more than ten years before this incident. She joined the NAACP in 1943, and members quickly elected her secretary because it was a woman's job, and she remained in that position until 1957. During her tenure as secretary, she helped investigate the gang rape of Recy Taylor and later helped organize a protest for the rape of a Black woman, Gertrude Perkins, by two white police officers. She was also a member of the League of Women Voters. In 1955, she was an advisor to the NAACP youth committee.

Another rarely mentioned part of Rosa Parks's story is her experience riding on nonsegregated public transportation. In 1944, she briefly worked at the Maxwell Air Force Base in Montgomery. Because the base was federal property, she rode on the integrated trolley on base. She said later that her experience on that trolley opened her eyes to what life would be like without segregation (Theoharis 2013, 17, 50–51).

In other words, Rosa Parks did not act unconsciously. She made a determined choice not to move from that seat.

In *Rosa Parks: My Story*, she said people thought she gave up her seat because she was old and tired. "I was not tired physically, or no more tired than I usually was at the end of a working day. I was not old, although some people have an image of me as being old then. I was forty-two. No, the only tired I was was tired of giving in" (Parks and Haskins 1999, 116).

In a 1992 interview with National Public Radio's Lynn Neary, Parks recalled:

> I had not planned to get arrested. I had plenty to do without having to end up in jail. But when I had to face that decision, I didn't hesitate to do so because I felt that we had endured that too long. And the more we gave in, and the more we complied with that kind of treatment, the more oppressive it became… I did not want to be mistreated. I did not want to be deprived of a seat I had paid for. And it was just time… There was an opportunity for me to take a stand to express the way I felt about being treated in that manner (Neary 1992).

Ms. Parks was an instigator. She saw inequity and quietly did something about it. Her refusal to move sparked other people to action. Granted, in her life as a southern Black woman, she had seen that force did not always move people to action, so she knew yelling wasn't going to work. She needed to be calm and quiet, with nerves of steel. Yelling, as Claudette Colvin found out, could have deleterious effects.

It struck me that creating a movement doesn't start with planning to start a movement. People who end up starting grassroots change are just doing what they can to solve an injustice. Their actions, however tiny, can motivate others. The ripples move outward and get bigger and bigger, becoming the movement. The actions of the other women spurred Rosa Parks on. But ultimately, Claudette, Aurelia, Susie, Mary Louise, Jeanetta, and Rosa were just pebbles. Their tiny actions caused the ripples that led to the 1960s civil rights movement.

These women were aware of the issue of civil rights. They lived with inequity and wanted to do something about it. They didn't refuse to move because they thought they would be famous. They chose their course of action because it was a way of causing discomfort and, therefore, creating change. I am excited to see Claudette Colvin has been drawing more attention in recent years. Seeing the other instigators behind the more famous one is important to see where the ripple originated.

Many events start out as small grassroots movements: the Freedom Riders, the Women's March, and Occupy Wall Street, to name a few. Some fizzle out, some contribute to other movements, and some just keep going. The human ability to influence change fascinates me. When we pay attention, articulate the discrepancies, and develop nontraditional solutions, our actions can motivate others. This is the spirit of the instigator.

CHAPTER 4

TYPES OF INSTIGATORS

So many people in my life have illustrated different aspects of instigation. When you surround yourself with people who play these roles in your life as well, you just have to pay attention. They don't call attention to themselves unnecessarily. These aren't people who set out to do something big. Rather, they are aware of a need and find a creative way to fulfill it to benefit others. Let me give you some examples.

- The Curator

My grandmother was a force. I didn't realize that when I knew her.

My first memories of her are a lavender bathrobe, soft skin, and the smell of Coty face powder. She was tall, imposing, and stylish. Friday club, volunteering, and puttering about in the garden filled her days. We would have tea in the afternoon, during which she always used the good china and silverware.

But she was also someone who got stuff done.

Born in 1910, Hatty lost her mother at seven years old, becoming an independent creature. Her father worked long hours at the family's insurance company. Their housekeeper, Aunt Jane, was very practical but not very demonstrative, so she took over the emotional care of her five-year-old brother. Without the direction of a nanny or mother figure, Hatty chose clothing that was comfortable, not fashionable. Her father encouraged her curiosity and love of learning, which also went against the norm. Not only was she unconventional in her behavior, but by the time she was thirteen, she had reached her full height of six feet. Little kids would follow her home from school, teasing her about being a giant. Although hurtful, it led to her strong passion for supporting the underdog.

In 1930, Hatty went to art school, Académie Julian, in Paris. She stayed for two years, finished art school, and returned to Michigan. Jackson was very quiet after the hustle of Paris, so a year later, she visited an aunt in New York City. There, she met my grandfather, and they married in 1936.

In 1938, she and her new husband moved to Fogo Island, Newfoundland, to set up a medical practice. After two years, she started a library on the island with the books she brought with her. She once told me she only felt rich when surrounded by books. They moved back to Michigan in 1940, and my grandfather set up a practice there.

In the early 1960s, a local farm and farmhouse went up for sale. A German family named Realy had lived there since the 1850s when they first immigrated to the US.

Hatty decided it would be an amazing museum, and she set about creating The Waterloo Area Historical Society, raising money to buy the land and house to make the Waterloo Farm Museum. She spent the next few years talking to people about their experiences with the Realy family, requesting donations to the museum, and gathering money for the historical society. Her vision was to show a working farm—with everything set up to look like the family had just stepped out for a short while. She wanted to curate everyday items, not just valuable antiques. Washtubs, axes, and rug beaters hung in the entranceway, the table was set for dinner, and the woodburning stove worked. Working at the farm museum was my first job. I was a docent during the summer, taking folks on tours, showing how the butter churn worked, and selling things in the gift shop.

Sixty years later, the farm museum encompasses five other buildings, including a log cabin, a granary, a milk house, and a few barns, and the Waterloo Historical Society also owns a small one-room schoolhouse nearby. There are yearly celebrations such as Log Cabin Day, Pioneer Day, and Christmas at the Farm, and the local schools bring hundreds of kids in the fall.

I suppose Hatty's interest in art and her time at art school helped form her desire to curate items and display them. By the time she started the museum, her four kids had grown up, and she needed to find purpose again in her life.

But she had no training in starting a museum or a nonprofit. She just had a desire to do something to enrich her community. She didn't just say they needed to create the museum. She talked to people on the street, at the grocery, and at her church. She was persistent and dogged. Hatty would buttonhole people in the grocery. "Vern, I heard you have one of the old threshing machines from the Realy house. You surely aren't using it anymore. Can you bring it over to the farm?" She would attend meetings all over the county and explain the importance of remembering what the folks who created our community did to keep it alive. Then she'd leave with pockets full of checks and promises of help.

Her desire to shed light on the ordinary lives of everyday people was integral to creating the museum. She loved talking to people and asking them about their childhoods, grandparents, and traditions. She wanted to know how they used different tools and what handed-down recipes people had. Hatty would go to estate sales and auctions. She would persuade people to donate items and then ask them to come work at the museum. To maintain the house and outbuildings, the Waterloo Historical Society would have weekly work days in the summer that culminated in a potluck. This community involvement only strengthened the connections with those who volunteered, and the museum became a point of pride.

Although much of her life was unconventional, it was set in a framework of tradition. She kept house, raised her children, went to church, and fulfilled the social obligations of being the doctor's wife. But underneath, her desire to learn and be aware was always there. If she saw something needing doing, she did it. She didn't ask or worry about the what-ifs. She just forged ahead as if written into her DNA.

• The Educator

I knew of him before I met him. My friend Meg previously taught with him for years. When she spoke about Don Tassie, it was always with love and affection, and maybe a little exasperation. He ran the alternative school in Jackson, Michigan, and was known as a great administrator, a wonderful teacher, and a caring person.

We first met at a conference in May of 1995. I had graduated from Eastern Michigan University the year before with a teaching certificate and was looking for something else besides substitute teaching. Meg dragged me along to the annual Michigan Alternative Educators Organization (MAEO) conference for the sole purpose of helping me find a job. It started out like any other conference—a keynote speaker, a dinner of dried chicken drenched in some kind of sauce, and a list of workshops and other speakers lined up for the next day. There were awkward conversations with the other people at the table. I had subbed in an alternative school and really enjoyed it, so I had something to contribute to the discussion. But mostly, I listened.

Let me tell you—alternative ed teachers are the most uninhibited people I have ever met. When the room darkened and the DJ came out, no one was sitting down. My theory is that since they deal with so much heaviness all the time, they need a place to release.

Don is thirty years my senior. At the time, I thought it amazing a fifty-four-year-old had so much energy. Now that I'm fifty-four, I'm not so surprised! He was on the dance floor almost the entire night before heading to another dance bar that wasn't in the hotel. Meg and I followed along with his entourage. We shut down that bar and headed to someone's suite at the conference hotel. It was three in the morning, and we sat on the floor in the packed room with our backs against the wall. Don and Laura, another alternative ed teacher, got into a discussion about teaching theories. Don was starting a charter high school called the da Vinci Institute in August. He was so full of excitement about the plans he had. It was the first year of charter schools in Michigan, and there were few constraints. It was a blank slate. Sitting there, listening to Don and Laura talk about the educational theories of Madeline Hunter, who created the instructional theory into practice teaching model, and William Glasser, an American psychiatrist who developed choice theory, I knew I was with the people I wanted to work with.

Working in public schools had frustrated Don immensely. He wanted to do what was right for *kids*, which was not necessarily what the state mandated. He believed kids needed to find a spark, something that made them excited to learn. He wanted them to like learning for learning's sake, not because they needed to get a math or science credit.

Don had an interest in making sure kids knew the basics. All classes would start the day with ten minutes of essential skills. We would go over simple math problems, talk about the differences between the words "they're," "there," and "their," and explain cloud formations.

The school also wanted to focus on how the students felt about themselves, about others, and about education. They emphasize relationship building, self-esteem, and caring for others. Teachers learned about their students and their students' families. We knew who was couch surfing, who was living with their grandparents, and who probably didn't get breakfast. We wanted da Vinci to be a place where they felt comfortable and loved so they could become successful adults.

A large part of the da Vinci Institute was experiential. We would take students on field trips to auto factories, to airlines, and to construction sites so they could get excited about a career path. They would talk to those on the factory lines or those in charge of the construction sites and learn that geometry was important in figuring out how to do those jobs. When we got back to school, the kids had an unprecedented interest in learning geometry because they had seen it in the real world, and someone who wasn't a teacher had explained how necessary it was.

Traditional school requirements don't take into consideration what the student wants to do or whether they feel invested at all. A student takes algebra because it's the next on the list of what they need before college. Often, the everyday applications go unmentioned, or if they are, the student can't comprehend them because they haven't been in that situation. Teachers from other schools thought da Vinci wasn't a *real* school because we didn't teach things in the same, linear fashion.

Don started da Vinci with the idea that asking forgiveness was preferable to asking permission and based it all on the premise of doing the best for the students—the best learning environment, the best emotional environment, and the best curriculum. Much of what I incorporated into my life as an instigator, I learned from Don.

• The Advocate

Julia Miller looks like an anarchist wearing tight red plaid pants with straps hanging down, black zippers in strange places, and a black Misfits T-shirt with the neck cut out. Her hair could be black with red, pink, or green tips and usually tucked up under a black hat. She wears brightly colored eyeshadow under owlish glasses and perfectly applied lipstick in either black or red.

I can't remember where I met her the first time. I think she had started doing distributions to the local homeless population and was thinking about creating an official Punks With Lunch chapter. My nonprofit Helping Women Period was just three years old and chugging along wonderfully. I offered to sit down with her and help her with the nonprofit paperwork.

We scheduled a meeting at a local restaurant. When I walked in, four or five people were at the table: Julia, her partner Martin, and a few other people who helped with distribution. We sat down, and Julia told me they had been feeding people in the park, and the city was cracking down on them. They needed to make the sandwiches in an approved kitchen with health and safety protocols. Martin, a true anarchist, wanted just to keep going the way they had been and "screw the government." Julia was more pragmatic. If they got nonprofit accreditation, they could raise more money, become established, and do more for the people they wanted to help. She cajoled Martin into agreeing to file the paperwork by suggesting that by playing along with the government's requirements, they would be doing what the government didn't expect.

Julia is a radical at heart. She has helped shape the Lansing Punks With Lunch group into a major force in our community. During her distributions of food and other basic necessities at the parks, she got to know several of her regular clients. Many of them were addicts, and as a former drug addict, she wanted to support them in their journey in a way she needed but never got in those earlier days. Looking into harm reduction practices, she found what she needed. You can't shame addicts into quitting drugs, but you can help them do drugs more safely with a needle exchange, nonjudgmental medical information and counseling, and making sure they know how to use Narcan. Julia could get a grant to run the Harm Reduction arm of Punks With Lunch and quit her day job. She implemented free Narcan vending machines throughout the city and is still saving lives on a regular basis.

One way she could reach so many people and run her organization is due to The Fledge and Jerry Norris. The Fledge is a local community center where Julia offices.

Jerry is the owner, architect, and instigator behind this organization, which is so much more than just a community center. He lives and breathes his philosophy of radical acceptance (accepting what is not under your control and embracing what is happening now in a nonjudgmental way). Jerry started The Fledge after his eldest daughter died of a heroin overdose. He wanted to give back to the community that supported him during that time, and he wanted a way to help those who felt like they were alone and didn't know where to turn.

The Fledge is always evolving. When I first met Jerry, they had just moved into an old church. The sanctuary had the pews moved to the side. Pieces of artwork in various stages of completion were leaning against the back of one pew, a painted mural in progress was where the altar used to be, and fish swimming were in the baptismal font. Jerry led me to the fish, explaining the self-sustaining ecosystem. The fish ate from the plants floating on top, and the plants exchanged oxygen for carbon dioxide to help the fish breathe.

A group of high school kids who stopped by after school regularly had programmed an Arduino to test the pH of the water. If the pH was high, the lights in the sanctuary turned purple. If the pH was low, the lights would glow red. In another corner, a few people sat around a couple of computers, and Jerry told me they were working on applying for jobs, looking up their warrants, or trying to file for expungement.

We walked down the stairs to see handwritten words of love and encouragement covering the walls. The basement was stuffy and close, with a clothing rack filled with jackets pushed to one side, a large table set up with a few sewing machines in the middle, and a pile of Bernie for President signs in the corner under a six-foot-tall papier-mâché mushroom. There was a kitchen with two refrigerators. The hope was to make this into a commercial kitchen so they could have kids help make food to take home. Many of those who hang out here after school come from one-parent families, and they need to learn basic skills to take care of themselves and their siblings.

Another room in the basement had walls covered with acoustic panels and a small table with a few microphones and headphones. This is where Jerry hosts his podcasts and other groups record music. Outside The Fledge, they have a farm stand with free produce and two old refrigerators to hold eggs and meat. Anyone could come and grab food. They don't care if someone takes it all. The radical acceptance philosophy says, "They must have needed it." But people are usually circumspect in what they take. The yard is now a garden, and there's a little free pantry next to the sidewalk that holds tiny pieces of art.

Jerry is an instigator. He looks at the problems in our community and tries to solve them in a different way. We had a cold snap this past winter. The temps were sub-zero. Jerry opened up The Fledge as a warming center for a week. He had the fire marshal walk through to give approval. He saved people's lives that week. The city, which hadn't opened any new warming centers, got upset with him and fined him for not pulling the correct permits. Jerry shrugged this off. His reasoning was if the city wasn't going to take care of the vulnerable, someone had to, and he had the opportunity and the means.

Both Jerry and Julia are prime examples of the advocate instigator. They identify and advocate for the needs of people who don't have enough influence to advocate for themselves, and they do this because they want to help the community. Neither of them look for accolades, and they realize they can't help everyone. Their goal is to help the person who is right in front of them. They are wonderful people, and I feel so lucky to know them.

- The Networker

Paul runs a video company specializing in telling the stories of nonprofits. He's created three videos for my organization. Two were informative videos used for marketing and grants, and the third was my TEDx Talk. He knows how to tell a story with film.

I met Paul officially at a traditional networking event—one of those early morning things with bad coffee and stick-on name tags. He talked about his video business, and I talked about Helping Women Period. We were friends with each other's friends, and it was natural to gravitate toward each other. He also knew many people and was so good at making sure everyone knew everyone else. Paul was good at creating connections because he was aware, paid attention, and knew even though the connection might not do anything for him personally, it would benefit the community.

A few years before COVID-19, he was one of the founders of a networking group called The Drinking Lunch. The group would meet every third Wednesday at one p.m. at a different bar or restaurant. It was a different kind of networking meeting—not coffee, not eight am. Usually, it would run into happy hour, and people would talk far into the evening. It was so fun, but then it fizzled, like many groups did, during COVID-19. It's one of those things that is not the same on video!

He and his friends helped start The Drinking Lunch because they were tired of traditional business networking meetings. Instead, they wanted to meet different people in different surroundings. Many networking groups are held in the early morning or at lunch. They require dues or that you spend a certain amount of money each month with the other businesses in the group. Such networking groups tend to become cliquish.

The Drinking Lunch was fun. The name sounded like it came from a mid-century modern TV show. There was an element of playing hooky with different people, different companies, and different kinds of interactions. Supporting local businesses, they made connections that couldn't have happened in a traditional networking group. Where else would a sculptor meet with a small retail store owner and a passionate recycler and create a neighborhood festival that spotlighted sculptures made from recycled metals? That festival, ScrapFest, has now been going strong for eight years!

At lunch, Paul told me a bit about a contest he's starting—Taco the Town. It's taco cook-off with traditional taco trucks and traditional and nontraditional restaurants (BBQ, Korean, and more). They plan to hold it in a local park in September, with musical acts and performances. All proceeds will benefit the local Hispanic Chamber of Commerce. He lit up when he told me about the family band he had booked for earlier in the day and then the other, louder bands for the evening.

This kind of talent for networking is a trait of the instigator. The ability to be aware of what is going on around you, of what the needs are, and how you can connect them is essential. The instigator doesn't do this for accolades or their own personal benefit necessarily but for the good of the community and the betterment of all. Also, instigation doesn't have to create sweeping, immediate change. Often, those little changes, like the first domino, can lead to so much more.

CHAPTER 5

COLLABORATION

Sometimes, for instigation to really work, you need some help. Working with other people, groups, and companies can be rewarding and move the needle further than you thought possible.

CROSSING WATER

Michael Hood is a self-described crotchety old curmudgeon. You could mistake him for a French-Canadian voyageur of old—round glasses, layers of clothing, a red stocking cap, and a disdain for modern conveniences. He still has a flip phone and abhors texting. He is also one of the most selfless people in the world. He has a social work background, takes people adventuring (winter camping, canoe trips, and the like), and is a perpetual volunteer and problem solver. What he lacks in finesse, he makes up in sheer determination.

The first time I worked with him was at the Cristo Rey Community Center Thanksgiving Meal. He sourced frozen turkeys, cajoled people to cook them at home, and made pans of mashed potatoes, corn, stuffing, gravy, and other sides, all cooked and prepared in-house by hand. He signed up servers, front-of-house workers, and delivery drivers. In our final year together, we served over eight hundred meals, with about 350 patrons coming through the doors for our sit-down dinner. Our remaining staff delivered another 450 meals out into the community, actually outpacing the in-house meals for the first time.

The intent was to treat all the people who came in like family, which is exactly how it felt. It did not feel like a soup kitchen. Instead, it had the atmosphere of a fine restaurant with all the dignity and amenities associated with one, including live music, menus in English and Spanish, waiters, and a maître d'. They served everyone in a comfortable and respectable sit-down-style restaurant.

One day, a few months later, he called me up and asked if I wanted to help build a ramp. An elderly veteran, John, who lived on the south side of town, was in a wheelchair now after having a diabetes-related amputation and couldn't get out of his house. Michael had spoken with John's sister, and she was at her wit's end. She couldn't afford to pay someone to build the ramp and couldn't physically help her brother out of the house.

Meanwhile, the local group that usually volunteered for ramp building was booked solid. Michael had talked a few carpenters into helping and donating the materials. He needed people to come to lift and tote things.

I had never built a ramp before. I knew Michael just a little and a few of the other people on the team even less. It was March in Michigan. The wind was bitter, and the snow was threatening. We showed up at nine in the morning on a Saturday and got to work, clearing debris around the front of the house, unloading the truck, and figuring out where the electrical outlets were.

There were some moments of indecision. Should it be attached to the house or not? Should there be tread on the ramp so when things are wet, it won't be slick? The goal was to have it done before lunch, and we did it. A landing right outside the door so John could open the door and close it again. A ramp that went down the side of the house but didn't go too much into the drive. The carpenters had to go to a paying job, so they left as soon as they drove the last nail. The rest of us cleaned up and sat around the back of Michael's red pickup, with the canoe on top, and talked about the build. I'm pretty sure no one pulled any permits. Michael is one to do and then ask forgiveness later. John was happy. He could get out of his house now and have more freedom, and we were bone tired but satisfied.

Michael has a way of pulling you in and making you want to help right alongside him. His sense of justice and injustice is a driving force in the choices he makes. In 2014, the Flint water crisis came to the public eye. The lead water pipes were leaching into the water systems, causing illness and injury, especially to those with preexisting conditions and, most disturbingly, the city's children (Parks and Mantha 2015).

The crisis spared no one. The water corroded the faucets, toilets, washing machines, and showers. Fire trucks broke down because the insides of the pumps contained iron and lead deposits.

However, the worst thing was the overriding poverty. Many of the people of Flint couldn't afford to move somewhere else. They couldn't afford to buy new faucets, filters, or bottled water from the store. The affected neighborhoods consisted of resettled refugees, migrant workers, and others with minimum-wage jobs, a poor grasp of English, and nowhere to go. Flint had a large population of at-risk and underserved people who didn't trust the police or the government. They couldn't read the notices written in English either (US Census Bureau 2018–2022).

Groups forty-five minutes away in Lansing started holding bottled water drives, renting U-Haul trucks, meeting in a grocery store parking lot, and filling the trucks with trays of bottled water. They would drive them to Flint and drop them off at the fire station. This drove Michael to distraction. He knew the folks who really needed the water weren't going to go to the fire station, or they lived too far away to walk to the station and carry the water back home. He started going to Flint and distributing bottled water from house to house. He took along a few other social workers who spoke Spanish. Around that time, the government started giving out water filters to attach to the tap, but no aid agencies or other humanitarian groups were willing or able to go inside homes to help the residents install the water filters correctly. So, Michael's teams started bringing tools and skilled workers to install the filters.

Although he knew he was helping as many as he could, it felt like it wasn't enough. He started a group called Crossing Water, staffed by crews called the Rapid Response Service Teams, or RRSTs (Pennington 2017). He gathered volunteers via Facebook and word-of-mouth prior to scheduling weekly events. Every team had a social worker and someone who spoke Spanish. He trained all team members not only to install the filters but also to teach residents how to install and check their own filters, a critical skill set when dealing with lead in the drinking water.

The RRSTs did thousands of home visits and explained to the residents that boiling water wouldn't remove the lead but would only serve to concentrate it, making the water even more toxic. This was indeed a critical piece in the intervention since residents had no choice but to rely on bottled water for drinking and making baby formula. Even though water is in their name, Crossing Water teams always saw their mission as being one far greater and bigger than the water crisis. Flint was already a city in need due to years of long-term unemployment, willful neglect, and little economic opportunity, which created a whole host of intractable urban problems besieging this beleaguered population of underserved citizens and families.

Crossing Water found ways to get new appliances for these families and bigger vessels of water and organized other help such as food, bottled water, baby formula, clothing, and bus passes as well. They even made sure every home with young children received age-appropriate kids' books. The illiteracy rate in Flint was disturbingly high at 10 percent, which added to the problem of reading instructions for how to put in the water filters and other important written information from the government on how to manage the crisis virtually impossible for some families (Flint and Genesee Literacy Network 2018).

Every weekend for the first few months, the RRSTs would deploy. They eventually pulled back to once weekly and, after a few more months, managed to have teams go out monthly depending on staffing availability. Michael found a church to host them so they could work without having to move supplies back and forth from Lansing and Ann Arbor. The pandemic didn't slow them down. They just donned PPE and kept going.

The state attorney general's office also subpoenaed Crossing Water to testify in federal court to attest the so-called effectiveness of the state's response to the water crisis (House 2023). After Crossing Water shared their deep and well-documented data on their home visits with the court, and Michael himself testified, the court found in favor of the residents. They found responses to the water crisis by the state of Michigan and the city of Flint to be meager, inadequate, and ineffective at best, falling far short of their obligations to the residents there. It was not only a huge win for the families of Flint but also for the work and ongoing efforts of the dedicated and hardworking, 100 percent volunteer Rapid Response Services Teams.

After seven years, Crossing Water ended most of the humanitarian relief work in Flint, but the effects of the humanitarian relief and crisis intervention that Michael instigated continue. He didn't ask permission. He didn't turn away and say it wasn't his problem. He and Crossing Water created new interventions and solutions no one else was attempting and implemented new types of interventions and emergency responses in times of dire crisis. No one paid him to do this. It was just what needed to be done. He not so secretly hopes and believes other aid and humanitarian groups, big and small, will copy Crossing Water's innovative and new model for crisis intervention and humanitarian work and use it unsparingly to answer the call of other communities in crisis and to help other families in need.

Being an instigator means collaborating to get the job done. Engaging others in the work encourages creativity and increases awareness of the issue. Crossing Water could serve more people in ways other than giving out bottles of water. They developed nontraditional solutions. The affected Flint families will feel the ripples these teams created for years.

PART 2

If you think you are too small to make a difference,
you haven't spent a night with a mosquito.

—AFRICAN PROVERB

CHAPTER 6

HOW I BECAME AN INSTIGATOR

In the late sixties, I was born in a commune in Colorado. My parents were hippies—long hair, beaded leather jackets, a motorcycle, and disdain for authority. They were both physician's kids who had graduated from a small private college in Michigan with degrees in biology.

My mother was an artist. She looked at things in a different way on purpose. She was calm yet excited about nature. I remember her calling me over when I was five and showing me a handful of sand under a magnifying glass. She wanted me to look at the colors and be amazed at the infinitesimal world she held.

My dad was an environmentalist who dreamed of living off the land. He valued logic, philosophy, and questioning. One of his favorite pastimes was engaging in long, rambling conversations about reality versus illusion. His insistence on questioning was frustrating and valuable at the same time.

Both Mom and Dad wanted to parent differently than they had been. In the late forties and early fifties, most parenting was authoritarian—*Father Knows Best* and all that—especially in a doctor's family. There was no room for discussion, feelings, or new ideas. My father, the youngest of four and the only boy, was left to his own devices as a kid. He'd take two bologna sandwiches and a thermos of water and walk in the woods until dinner time.

My mother was the eldest of five girls. She strove to be good: a good student, a good daughter, and a peacemaker. She did what her parents told her to do when they told her to do it.

In contrast, my childhood consisted of a lot of talking about feelings, ideas, and behavior. I only remember my parents grounding me once. If they told me to do something, they explained why or what the end result would be. If I didn't want to or disagreed, they would listen to my reasons, and we would talk more. There was no threat of retaliation or worry about punishment, just a lot of self-reflection.

In one of my earliest memories, when I was around three years old, Mom warned me about the stove and how hot it was. She told me about what would happen if I touched the stove, what burns were, how they affected your skin, and how to treat them. She let me bring a chair over and stir the eggs, so it wasn't a scary situation. Later, if I went near the stove, she'd just have to say, "Lizzy, remember about the stove," and I'd steer clear of it.

Looking back, I realize my childhood taught me about the value of internal motivation and a disdain for authoritarian behavior. I don't remember much rebellion in my teen years, except for sneaking candy and soda pop because we didn't have sugar in our house. Part of that lack of pushing away was because I knew others valued and supported me, and I was in charge of *myself.*

As I started working and putting myself through college, I found I did not like confrontation or someone telling me what to do. I also didn't want to sit there with impotent rage when seeing someone wronged. One day, in an intro to linguistics class, our professor refused to give us a study guide or even a list of what we would be covering on the first test. During the break, I asked my classmates what they thought of the frustrating situation. What were our options? When we got back into class, other people started asking him why. We ended up having a great conversation, and the professor relented as he gave us a list of what might be on the test.

I began to seek out experiences like these, where my willingness to acknowledge a common need was an opportunity to rally people and partner with them toward a common goal. Later, I would come to think of this as instigator leadership, a style of leadership that isn't loud or dominating but caring and cooperative; leadership that is willing to initiate but doesn't need to be in charge, creating change from within.

The year after college, I subbed in an alternative school, and it was glorious. The school served breakfast sandwiches every morning, and there were no bells. There was coffee available for anyone. We could teach inside or out, and the kids had staggered starts, so it was easy to spend time with each individual and go over the work for the day. I decided this was the kind of place where I wanted to work, so I went to the MAEO conference, and a month later, I was sitting in an interview with Don Tassie, who was starting a brand-new charter school, called the da Vinci Institute, based on manufacturing.

Charter schools were still a new development. The requirement of each charter was to focus on a different skill area, such as science, performing arts, or mechanical skills. Since we were in a community supported by several manufacturing businesses, it made sense to focus on that. Our school would use new educational theories and practices, and we would all work together to ensure our students were successful.

We started in 1995 in an unused wing of the local community college. They hired me the day before school started, and I walked into a room without desks. They were back-ordered, so we had to create an alternative plan. We rented some tables from a nearby party supply store. They were heavy and made of laminated wood, and the tops were peeling. We covered them with butcher paper and handed out crayons—to high school students. This was just the beginning of dealing with education in a different way.

Our goal was to teach kids, to treat them as people, and not use coercion to achieve an end goal. This was a radical departure from the student treatment in traditional schools. The first thing we wanted to do was to change the way they thought of school. We learned their names on the first day, played ice-breaking consensus-building games, went by our first names, provided breakfast, and didn't do anything traditional except take attendance.

Our rules were few: be respectful, reasonable, and responsible. Simple, yet surprisingly effective. When someone exhibited behavior that wasn't appropriate, we would take them aside and ask: "Hey, was that respectful?" And listen. "Was it reasonable?" And listen. "Was it responsible?" And listen. Then we'd ask, "What do you think needs to happen?" Kids are so much harder on themselves than our consequences would ever be.

For instance, Jack kept interrupting during our town meeting, teasing another kid about his mohawk and just being loud. I asked him to come into the other room with me—and you could see him getting ready to argue with me. I said calmly, "Hey, Jack, what's going on? Do you know why I brought you in here?"

In sullen tones, Jack said, "Nothing. No." I waited a bit, not saying anything. "Well," he continued, "I was teasing Aaron about his hair. Who does that?"

"Jack, is that a respectful way to talk to someone?" I asked.

"No, but I really am curious about his hair. It looks uncomfortable."

"It may be uncomfortable. What would be a reasonable or respectful way to find out more about his hair?" I queried.

"Well, I suppose I could just ask."

"Do you think he'll want to answer based on how you treated him during town hall? Would you want to talk to someone who just called you dumb?"

"I guess I should apologize, and then maybe I can ask."

"Yes, Jack, that is a responsible way to deal with this situation. Thank you. Now go back to class."

We rarely carried out at-home suspensions and only occasionally did in-school suspensions because we wanted them to know we valued their education. They would miss so much if they weren't there. If their behavior interfered with the education of the others in the class, they would go do their work in the office with Don, the principal.

I didn't teach any English until November of that year. I assigned reflective writing and a few novels, plays, and poetry, but our focus was on creating the community. Every Friday started with breakfast for all. The teachers would cook pancakes and bacon or French toast. Afterward, there was town hall, where Don would talk a bit about what he enjoyed about the past week and what we could all improve on. We discussed issues from the past week and ideas about how to run the school, form clubs, and more. We ended every town hall with *warm fuzzies*—things people noticed that made them feel good, wanted, or safe.

They were definitely the halcyon days. Sure, we had tough kids considered *troublemakers* at their last school. A few had court-ordered ankle monitors. Some wore black leather jackets with silver spikes and band names painted with white out, unusual piercings, brightly colored hair, handmade tattoos, and lots of tight plaid pants with zippers at the ankles. Others were quiet, mousy kids who never fit in, or angry kids who didn't know why they were angry.

But they knew two things for sure: We loved them, and we wanted them to learn. So many of that first group of students had never had support and encouragement. They had never had someone in a place of authority who knew their name, who knew their story, who believed they could do good things, and who liked them as individuals. They had never been in a place that valued their individuality.

Two theories shaped our approach with students at da Vinci, drawn from Glasser's choice theory as found in his book *Reality Therapy.*

1. All human behavior is based on one of the following five basic human needs: love, power, fun, freedom, and survival.
2. Every individual has the power to control themselves but limited power to control others (Glasser 1975, 8–11).

Looking at these students through the lens of Glasser's choice theory helped us help *them* figure out how to navigate. Traditional schools hadn't given them the opportunity for choice or control, insisting they *follow directions, don't be late,* and *listen for the bells.* Boredom was part of the reason they were troublemakers. There was no room for them to be creative or to make decisions about themselves.

The students also lacked control in their lives at home. They were subject to the whims of parents caught in addiction, severe poverty, or depression. They were often responsible for younger siblings and sick parents. They often lacked food, shelter, or basic hygiene. They had been self-medicating for *years,* which included smoking, drugs, drinking—even cutting or other self-harm. During that first month, many of them were angry because we didn't do things like their other schools. We held them accountable for their actions. Is it reasonable? Responsible? Respectful? We gave them choices about what they could learn and about how to learn it. We made mistakes and owned up to them. We were transparent, vulnerable, and real.

There were heartbreaking times too. It's easier to fall back on known coping mechanisms when you are doing new, scary things. Or when you only get support at school and not at home. Or when you are working a few part-time jobs and going to school at the same time.

Learning to think in a whole new way is difficult, requiring patience and dedication. We had students who were in Narcotics Anonymous but relapsed. Some students were beyond our abilities. A pathological liar's hacking exploits brought the FBI to our door. One ended up in the hospital because of self-harm and an eating disorder. We had to expel a student who lived with his grandmother and brought a knife to school because of Michigan's zero-tolerance law.

Others persevered. These were creative kids who had finally found an outlet and people who supported who they really were or wanted to be; kids who were forging a new future that broke away from the generational trauma of poverty and abuse.

It was scary for the teachers too. We had never done this before, and being comfortable with chaos was sometimes difficult for the experienced teachers on our staff accustomed to a more corporate structure. In traditional schools, teachers relied on their reputation and authority to gain respect. At da Vinci, the educators were partners in learning. There was no instant respect, and we didn't expect that. When they came into the school, they would mention friends or family or talk about their new car. Often, the teachers would slide back into their traditional teaching methods as a defense, but they learned the traditional methods didn't work anymore.

I learned to be an instigator here. I wanted any change in the lives of my students to come from within—not from a place of authority. If it came from within, the kids would have more buy-in because it was not someone telling them what to do.

Instigators are great at consensus building. I learned a lot about asking questions. What if? What do you want? What would that look like? Who would benefit? Who would suffer? How could we make it inclusive? How could we do that and have it fit in with the state requirements or the law?

I also learned about sitting back and letting kids think or stew. I'd answer noncommittedly or just wait and let the silence get heavy. They learned I wouldn't give them the answer and that I didn't have a specific answer in mind. I valued their thought, their input, and their ownership.

It was challenging work. But this experience was life-changing for me. My students pushed me in many ways. They needed boundaries but also freedom. My job was to teach them how to communicate their needs in clearer ways. They needed to know I was there to pick them up when they failed and that I would always care for them. I wanted them to know how to ask questions and how to use confrontation as a tool, not a weapon. The best way to do that was to model the behavior I wanted them to learn. I learned how to redirect the conversations, how to listen to the subtext, and how to challenge them to think in another way.

We changed the lives of these students and gave them another way to look at the world. What would happen if more people changed their perspective about how the world works? What would it look like? How would it feel to live in a world with more creative problem-solvers? This is the world instigators will try to create.

CHAPTER 7

COMMUNITY

What makes community and connection? I started a Facebook group in one county, and it was wildly successful. I tried to replicate it in another county, and it failed spectacularly. The premises and rules were the same, but it just didn't gel that second time. Why did it fail? Because, in part, I didn't know the second community as well. I couldn't be an effective instigator.

In that second instance, I couldn't be an effective instigator because instigators need connection and community. Knowing people is the best way to get them on board. An old boss of mine used to say, "Everybody wants to be somebody; nobody wants to be a nobody." The more we know about others and the more aware we are of what is going on around us, the better equipped we are to solve the issues that affect us.

Everyone is looking for connection. It's an integral part of being human. Little kids are great at this. They sit down in the sandbox, look at the other kid, and say, "I like snails." The other kid will say, "I like red," and they will be friends for life.

We spend most of our formative years trying to force connections—what we wear, what we say, how we act—or trying to break out of the connections we have. This is partly because, as adults, it is our expectation to provide structure for our kids. We give them so many opportunities to learn and create connections. School, summer camp, playdates, and afterschool programs are great situations for kids to meet other kids and create friendships.

In adulthood, those opportunities are more limited and the stakes higher—and as such, these connections become harder as we get older. In our society, friendships have less value than romantic relationships. While there are numerous dating apps to facilitate romantic relationships, there are only a handful of apps for making friends. Moreover, unlike dating, there is no one to guide us in finding friends. We have to choose for ourselves where to go and decide if it's worth the risk of putting ourselves out there.

Communities are groups of people with a shared connection. It can be physical (like neighborhoods), spiritual (churches), intellectual (schools), or virtual. Let's take a look at a few places to create connections.

In 1999, I was on an online forum called Readerville. One of my favorite aspects of that group was a thread called Chattering. It was a place where the focus wasn't necessarily on books but on other things we had in common, such as recipes, relationships, the struggles with being a writer or a reader, or combining our work lives with our love of books. After Readerville closed down, a group of us, all women—the majority of whom were librarians—found another site to continue the Chattering thread. Even though we've been friends for more than twenty years, and I have only met a few in real life, we still "talk" weekly.

While writing this book, I found other communities that were helpful. I went to a writing group, which was nerve-wracking. I hadn't flipped the switch yet, not believing I could call myself a writer despite my passion. Everyone else in the group focused on poetry, screenplays, or short stories. I felt so out of it with my nonfiction thought leader book. We wrote together for about thirty minutes, and then folks started to share. Everyone who went before me was amazing. The guy who read just before I did had already published a few novels, and you could tell he loved the way words worked together. I didn't want to share, but I did. It was amazing! I received helpful feedback and decided I *could* call myself a writer.

I also went to a women's networking group called the National Association of Career Women (NACW). We started out every meeting with who we were, what we did, and what we were working on. I said my usual name and how to pronounce it, talked a bit about Helping Women Period, and mentioned I was writing a book about being an instigator. What a relief to have it out in the open! Afterward, so many people came up to talk to me about the book—to tell me stories about their experiences with change, leadership, and writing. It was very affirming.

So, what communities do you belong to? How do they help you be you?

We second-guess what others are looking for when we attempt to forge connections. Adults are great at introspection and gaslighting themselves when it comes to friendships. We don't take advantage of the luxury of enjoying the connection for what it is. Nor do we allow ourselves to be vulnerable and share—a pity.

However, like it or not, humanity has roots in connection. That is one reason the COVID-19 pandemic was so harmful. We jumped from an in-person connection to an online one, while a lot of the physical cues we relied on weren't as obvious via video. Once the quarantine lifted, many were desperate to go back to *normal*, yet the insular nature of that year changed a lot of us. Normal wasn't the same.

NETWORKING EVENTS
When we are at networking events, what do we do?

We shake hands, introduce ourselves, and mention something about what we do. This is because we want to find something of ourselves in others—a piece of common ground. It feels much more comfortable building a relationship if we have a starting place of shared interests.

ONLINE FORUMS AND GROUPS

We've all seen the warnings that our obsession with technology, and by association, social media, is ruining our ability to establish relationships. "Put down your phone!" is a common refrain, as is "Social media is a waste of time."

I have found, however, that amazing things can come out of technology. I have virtual friends all over the world whom I've never met physically. My horizons expanded, and I have learned so much! In fact, if it weren't for technology and social media, I would not be doing what I'm doing today.

NOT YOUR MOTHER'S NETWORKING GROUP

In October 2015, I ran into my friends Beth and Yvonne at a local restaurant and sat down with them. Beth was a writer, Yvonne a database expert and administrator, and I was working for a fledgling nonprofit. I told them a bit about what I was doing and all the places I would go that were looking for volunteers. Yvonne talked about how draining and frustrating her corporate job was because she had to keep her lifestyle secret. Even in 2015, being a lesbian was tough. We talked about networking and how most groups we knew required payment to join. Most consisted of white men and women who wore suits and high heels to work every day. Just then, our friend Toni walked by.

Toni sat down, took a sip of her coffee, and sighed. "I was at a women's networking conference all week."

"How cool!" said Beth. "What did you learn?"

"I learned that women's networking is a sham." Toni shook her head. "The speakers were all men. There were no women speaking."

Shockingly, the table was silent. Men at a women's networking event? That is not good. We knew plenty of amazing women in our community who could have contributed.

We decided to create a Facebook group—a local women's networking group that was nontraditional, a safe space for women, a place for creatives, introverts, and people who worked out of their homes to virtually meet and share ideas and information. Our vision was to create an environment that served the same purpose as the fence in our mothers' backyards but different, newer, and fresher. We called it Not Your Mother's Networking Group (NYMNG). People who felt out of place at traditional networking events found themselves welcomed with open arms. Those women we knew would be good connections.

For the first six months, we hosted monthly in-person networking potlucks. We had a special room for introverts that was quiet, with low light, colored pencils, and paper. As people brought finger foods, we offered drinks, introduced the group, and expressed our hope for how it would work. A few times, we held a kind of speed dating event, where everyone sat at a long table (about twenty-five people per side) and had the chance to tell the person across from them their elevator pitch for their business.

After two minutes, Yvonne would blow a whistle, and another person would talk for two minutes. At the next whistle, one side would move down a seat, and it would start again. It was a fabulous way of honing your elevator speech and getting to know the businesses of everyone in the community.

I got to know so many amazing entrepreneurs: artists, delivery services, and volunteers, as well as people who worked in traditional offices but were LGBTQIA+ or women of color. We wanted to be as inclusive as possible and to promote and lift each other up. We moderated all posts to ensure the vibe was upbeat. If someone wanted to talk about a bad experience with a company, we would ask them to first talk to the company before addressing the attorney general. We would not let a negative post in on its own, but people were welcome to talk about their experiences as comments on other posts.

We allowed women who lived or worked within twenty miles of our city to join. To gain acceptance, people had to answer three questions and promise to lift each other up and not put each other down. The scope has changed since we started. It's more of a pink Google now: Where's the best doctor, cake maker, or place to eat? There are job postings and volunteer postings. We created a few spin-off groups to help lessen the load of the main discussion page: NYMNG Parenting to discuss all things kid related; NYMNG Marketplace for selling individual items; NYMNG Travel for info outside of our area; and NYMNG Business Owners to discuss best business practices, how to market more effectively, and hiring and firing.

With more than twenty-one thousand members, sixteen thousand of whom are active on a weekly basis, the care and feeding of this group are important. As one of two volunteer admins, I spend about one hour to one and a half hours a day on that site, accepting members, approving posts, resolving conflicts, commenting, posting anonymous posts for people, teaching how to use the search box, and so on.

It can be a slog. You would not believe what people think is appropriate to share with twenty-one thousand of their closest friends. The admins work hard to maintain a drama-free environment. We preapprove all posts, so that helps keep things focused.

We have ten rules, the first of which is to be respectful. Remember kids in the sandbox? Sometimes, there's a kid who comes over and kicks sand all over the two who are having a delightful chat about snails and the color red. That's when an admin will step in, remove the kicker, and help them find a sandbox that works for them. We could also teach them the rules of the current sandbox, and then they can stay. The power behind twenty-one thousand women is amazing. A member posted on January 25 at 11:39 a.m. asking for hand warmers and other items to keep some of Lansing's homeless population warm during the polar vortex. Within twenty-seven hours, she had gathered and handed out coats, blankets, snacks, clothes, boots, and hand warmers—all donated by members of NYMNG.

This group is different. Our purpose is to promote local businesses and lift each other up. People can ask about a good doctor or where to find a specific ingredient, or they can find people who want to go on a hike together or walk dogs. One of my favorite sayings is, "A rising tide lifts all boats." How can we improve our society if we leave some behind? We don't allow rudeness or bullying. We value the contributions of our members, so we don't allow terms like "cost an arm and a leg" or "break the bank." Diplomacy is the name of the game.

NYMNG has always been quietly supportive and humming along gently in the background. We don't advertise but instead suggest membership to people who might benefit. I've thought about how to move it off the Facebook and Meta platforms, but it would be harder to keep it a safe women and women-identified space.

Once again, the instigation came from being aware and paying attention to the needs of the community. Having no investment in the exact outcome was also important. The group evolved beyond a simple networking site. We now have separate groups to discuss parenting, travel, business ownership, our own marketplace, as well as the main group. Members must belong to the main group before joining the others. This way, we know they went through a vetting process. They live in the area, are women, and agree to the rules of lifting others up. Therefore, other members can find this a safe place.

It's been going on for almost nine years now. So many businesses have started in our group and gone on to be successful. Whenever I think about closing it down, I hear another success story. Not everyone is happy with what we do or how we do it, and it is difficult sometimes to be on the receiving end of criticism. I have to remind myself it's one person out of twenty-one thousand and not to take their comments personally. I know the structure of the group is good and our reasoning clear.

CHAPTER 8

HELPING WOMEN PERIOD

Amy Stephenson and I knew each other tangentially. Our kids went to the same school, and we passed each other in the hallways during drop-off and pick-up. We helped out in the classrooms and became Facebook friends.

One night in January 2015, at two a.m., we both reposted a social media post about the lack of menstrual products available for homeless women. This story tugged at us. It talked about using those horrid paper towels from the gas station or dirty socks as temporary pads. We messaged each other to talk about our surprise this was happening in the United States. We had donated cereal, bread, and soup to the local food pantries but never pads or tampons.

We had assumed the Women, Infants, and Children (WIC) program would provide the necessary products, including menstrual products, diapers, and formula. However, to our surprise, the program only offered formula. We realized we needed to take action, so we founded Helping Women Period to provide these essential products to those in need.

I call it an accidental nonprofit. This was just going to be a one-and-done event. We figured we would invite thirty of our closest friends to breakfast, ask for donations, maybe make $500, and then buy a couple of cases of pads online to donate to our local shelter. Easy peasy.

The local restaurant had room for just thirty people, so we created an event on Facebook and posted it on Sunday. By Tuesday of that week, we had to change the venue because more than one hundred people wanted to attend, and the restaurant was too small. On Thursday, we filed nonprofit paperwork because people from all over the world wanted to donate money, and we wanted to be as transparent as possible.

Three weeks later, we were standing in front of more than one hundred people looking at us, waiting for us to talk about pads and tampons and how they could help.

We didn't know what we were getting ourselves into at that first breakfast. We just wanted to change what had been happening. And the only way to instigate change is to make people a little bit uncomfortable. Talking about pads and tampons does make people uncomfortable, even when using more socially acceptable terms like *hygiene products*. And here we were, talking about periods and pads while people were eating.

But it worked. And people talked back, telling us stories of their first period, the time they leaked in class, and how embarrassing it was to sit on the side of the pool during gym class. Everyone knew why you weren't in the water.

The stigma was universal. Every menstruator in the room had a story laced with shame. Amy and I didn't want our daughters to go through that. We didn't want anyone in our community to go through that, so we decided to do what we could without a preconceived notion of what it would look like.

We raised money and started talking about this issue to everyone around us. And we started listening. We found groups who already had relationships with our target market and talked to them about providing menstrual products. The response was incredible. Providers and recipients met us with tears in their eyes. Schools, shelters, and food banks were ecstatic. Helping Women Period grew at an astonishing rate. In the first year, we distributed about 150,000 individual pads and tampons, which covered about 7,500 periods. In 2022, we distributed a total of 1.14 million pads and tampons (about fifty-seven thousand periods), and in 2023, we distributed more than two million menstrual products (about eighty-eight thousand periods). Since its inception, we've distributed more than six and a half million menstrual and incontinence products.

I don't have a degree in nonprofit management, nor do I have an MBA or a degree in women's studies. However, I have a strong desire to do what is good for my community and to fix the wrongs that have been going on for too long. When we started Helping Women Period, we had no idea what we were doing. We relied on information from friends who managed nonprofits, learned the hard way about supply chain management, and spent an inordinate amount of time researching period poverty and nonprofits online.

One thing I've realized recently is I have a hard time taking credit for all the hard work I've done, and I'm not totally sure why. Part of it is that I didn't start doing this for recognition. Period poverty is a solvable issue, affecting millions of people every month. Distributing pads and tampons is just taking care of a symptom. The true issue is complex. We need a livable wage, we need to discover new solutions for homelessness, and we need appropriate, medically accurate education in schools about menstruation and to start that education earlier. Eight-year-olds getting their period is no longer uncommon. Once I realized we were only taking care of the symptoms, I wanted to do more. I worked on an educational webinar about menstruation and tried to figure out what my next steps could be.

A phone call from my friend Beth Bowen interrupted my daydreaming. "Lysne, do you want to get together with some other groups to get rid of the tampon tax in Michigan?" Beth had talked to a group called Period Equity—a collection of lawyers who were suing the state of Michigan for having a tampon tax. They were interested in creating a coalition to help get the legislation passed. Of course I said yes!

We started by making a list of other groups who would be interested—some local, some state-wide, some national. Mission Menstruation, a period advocacy group out of Michigan State University, was just getting their start.

We reached out to Period.org, a national group that fights period poverty, and I Support the Girls-Detroit—a chapter of a national organization.

This was May 2021. Things were starting to open up again after the pandemic, but we were still cautious. Video calls, phone calls, and long emails helped in the planning. We decided on a two-part strategy: meet with legislators to stimulate political action; and host two events, a legislative action day and a rally at the capitol, to generate public awareness for the tax repeal.

Luckily, a few legislators had been championing tax repeal on menstrual products for years. We were able to drum up support for the already presented bill. We talked to anyone who would listen and some who weren't really interested. Unsurprisingly, the legislators behind this bill from the start were all women, and many of them were women of color. They had brought this bill to the floor for nine years running. It always died in committee. And who ran the various committees where the bill died? Men—people who did not have the lived experience of having a period.

I don't think there was any ill intent behind the lack of momentum. It was a combination of ignorance and embarrassment. Periods were *not* something discussed at the capitol. In fact, less than fifteen years before this, in 2012, the House floor removed Democratic State Representative Lisa Brown for saying *vagina*. "Mr. Speaker," she said during a debate about abortion legislation, "I'm flattered you're all so interested in my vagina, but no means no." Majority Floor Leader Jim Stamas (R-Midland) determined Brown's comments violated the decorum of the House and barred her from speaking for a one-day period.

"The war on women in Michigan is not fabricated," then-Senator Gretchen Whitmer stated at the time. "This is very real—and it comes at the highest levels of state government" (Skubick 2012).

So we advanced the tampon tax repeal with a double objective to a) educate those in charge, and b) get this bill passed.

An advantage we already had was that in May 2020, the federal government had passed the Coronavirus Aid, Relief, and Economic Security Act (CARES): a stimulus plan that addressed both emergency health care and financing for treatment and prevention of COVID-19. A provision in this piece of legislation classified menstrual products as essential medical devices for the IRS (CARES Act 2020). Previously, the FDA classified them as medical necessities, but the IRS didn't, so there wasn't a way for people to use HSA and FSA (pretax) funds to pay for them. Once the IRS got on board, however, those funds were able to go to menstrual products. Michigan tax law states essential items are nontaxable, so the IRS ruling should have already led to the repeal of the tampon tax in Michigan (MCL-Section 205.54g 1933). Period Equity was suing the state because they weren't in compliance, and soon, legislators from both sides of the aisle became interested.

One such legislator was Bryan Posthumus, a Republican who wanted to be a sponsor of the bill. "It's common-sense legislation," he said when testifying in front of the House Appropriations Committee. The women who championed this bill for years compromised and let him be the sponsor. Having men in the legislature supporting the bill and actually saying the words "menstrual products" and "pads and tampons" while testifying was a real step forward for the Michigan government!

Now, we had legislative support and a sponsor for the bill, so the next step was to hold a legislative action day. This would do two things: educate high school and college students about grassroots advocacy and period poverty, and introduce the students to the legislators who represented them. As I had never done any advocacy, I had no idea what this would entail. All I knew about bills I had learned from *Schoolhouse Rock*. But I did know about period equity, how the lack of period products affected those most vulnerable, and how the elimination of the tampon tax would help society as a whole.

Beth secured meetings with legislators, a place to meet, and speakers. I organized high school and college students and snacks. Students from all over Michigan came to the capitol for the event on October 6, 2020. We met in the morning, talked about the process a bill goes through in the government, and taught them how to talk to legislators. In the afternoon, we set up meetings with different legislators who represented the areas the students came from. We also had a film crew following us around. They were working on a full-length documentary called *Periodical*, which premiered at SXSW in March 2023. They had an interest in the tampon tax repeal here in Michigan. They came for the legislative action day and then came back three days later for the rally on October 9. They even returned the next year in February for the bill signing.

On the legislative action day, the film crew actually caused more consternation with the legislators than discussing periods! It took some negotiating to get the legislators to let the film crew follow us into their offices. Some of the legislators didn't want to let the crew in, and some allowed only b-roll footage filmed (extra footage without sound) but not the conversations. But the conversations went well. We let the students do most of the talking. Beth and I did the introductions and spoke a little about why we were there, then the students asked their representatives to support the bill.

Legislators were happy because they could listen to constituents and get some publicity photos. Students felt heard and like they contributed, and our coalition could get the message across.

The Michigan Senate Appropriations Committee invited me to testify the next day, October 7. There was a hush when you walked into the rooms where they make decisions. It wasn't just the carpeting. The ceilings were high, and you had to check in with the security guard. I found our lobbyist friends and sat down. It was hard to breathe. Some of the committee members were there already, and the rest came in slowly. I arrived ten minutes early, and it seemed like an eternity. I looked up when the secretary called our attention. Out of twelve members, there was only one Black person and one woman, and they were the same person. I let out my breath slowly. This might be harder than I expected.

Someone else was testifying about another bill before me. The committee called them up after the reading of the bill to sit in the box in front of them. After turning on the microphone, they said their piece. The head of the committee thanked them, and that was it. Soon, it was my turn. They read the bill and said they had a Zoom commenter. It was Posthumus, the senator who was sponsoring the bill. He spoke for a bit, and they invited me to the box. I remembered to turn on the mic and read my bit. I reminded myself to look up, breathe, and speak more slowly than I thought I should. I thanked them for their time and went back on shaky legs.

That was it. It was so much easier than I thought. They approved the bill and sent it to the Senate floor. They wrangled it there, delaying it for a few days because of larger issues. Once approved, they sent it on to the governor, who approved it wholeheartedly.

The intention of our rally, scheduled for that Friday, was to be an information rally but instead became a celebration. A bus full of college students from Ohio came up to help celebrate. It was a gorgeous day in October. The sun shone, and leaves skipped up the walk. We had speakers and sign-holders, and the documentary crew came back. TV film crews were also there, and there was a festive feeling. We won! What started out as a simple phone call had manifested into a bill that turned into law.

An instigator is an advocate. We see things that aren't safe, ethical, or fair and create innovative solutions. We don't need to bludgeon people over the head with our rhetoric. Quiet persistence, curiosity, and dogged determination are our hallmarks. I said yes to my friend Beth without knowing what I was getting into. I could have continued to distribute pads and tampons and never reached out to the legislators. However, I knew that eliminating the tampon tax would be a step toward a more equitable playing field and would improve my community.

At first, I was nervous about talking to legislators. I had preconceived notions that they were busy, important people who didn't have time to talk to regular people. I was so wrong. I'm sure there are some like that, but all the people I spoke with in the House and Senate were glad to hear from constituents and really listened when we spoke. If you want to make a change, talking to legislators is a great way to start. I would suggest writing down your talking points so you can control your emotions. Not that being emotional is a bad thing, but you don't want to walk out of the meeting and realize you never asked for the thing you went in there to ask. Being an instigator means letting yourself be uncomfortable, because change won't happen if people are happy where they are.

CHAPTER 9

BENDING TOWARD JUSTICE

When we worked on the tampon tax, a bill was proposed in the House, and the coalition I was working with educated those in the House and Senate about period poverty and the damage the tampon tax was creating. Some legislators were already passionate about the topic and willing to be supportive. Going into this situation, I had assumed women legislators would be as shocked as I had been at the statistics and excited about this opportunity to create parity in the schools. I had also assumed former teachers, people in the trenches who had taught and cared about kids, would want to do whatever they could to help those kids.

In hindsight, I should have asked my lobbyist what the procedure was and what to expect. I went into this idea of advocating for free products for public schools with one set of incorrect expectations.

What I didn't understand was how this time, we weren't asking for a bill. We were asking for a line item on the budget. We wanted five million dollars to supply all the school-age menstruators in the state who qualified for free and reduced lunch with a period kit of pads or tampons for nine months of school. According to the Alliance for Period Supplies (part of the National Diaper Bank), one in four school-age kids missed school during their periods in Michigan because they didn't have the products they needed (Alliance for Period Supplies 2021).

Missing school during every period would be at least nine days a year, and Michigan truancy laws kick in at ten absences, or 10 percent of the school year. (MCL-Section 380.1561). Students who qualify for free and reduced lunches are already behind and cannot afford to miss school.

When I first saw that statistic, I found it appalling. That is a lot of missed education. It seemed like a no-brainer to me. If they are missing school because they don't have menstrual products, let's give them products! But how? I can't drive all over the state to deliver pads. I was already working with forty schools in my own area. I started partnering with health departments to provide menstrual products to schools because they already had nurses and other health professionals in the schools.

But it still wasn't enough. I thought about the legislature. I contacted my friend Maureen, a lobbyist, and she offered to help us pro bono. We had worked together on the tampon tax repeal, and she knew everything worth knowing about the legislature. I explained what I wanted to do and gave her my cost analysis. That's when she started setting up meetings with senators.

Michigan was finally under Democratic control, so this was the perfect time to get our proposal in the budget. Legislators asked for a one-pager, a summary of what we were asking, why we were asking, and how we were qualified to ask. No one has asked for menstrual products for schools before, and our proposal was unlike any other similar proposal for other states. Other states were looking at free products in the restrooms—vending machines dispensing free pads and tampons or baskets with free products. Our proposal asked for twenty pads or twenty tampons to be distributed on a monthly basis to every menstruator in the schools who couldn't afford to purchase their own. We created our one-pager and started meeting with legislators.

Buoyed by Maureen's enthusiasm and my own eternal optimism, I went into the first meeting confident the Democratic senator, who was a woman and a former teacher, would be solidly behind the program. Quickly, I found disappointment. It embarrassed her to be discussing periods, however obliquely, in front of her male chief of staff. She kept apologizing to him, even though he was the one who had set up the meeting and read the one-pager. He knew what we were going to talk about. She said none of her constituents had ever mentioned this was a problem for them. I brought out the data and explained what we did, who we served, and who it affected. She countered this with her experience as a teacher: any time a student needed those products, she would send them to the office. Moreover, she added she had never had that kind of support when she was a student.

This flabbergasted me, as I had expected so much more understanding. Maureen jumped in and explained the amount of school these kids were missing, how the schools didn't have a line item in their budget for menstrual products, and how much her constituents would appreciate this. I brought up how people use products not meant for menstrual management, like T-shirts and socks, which opens them up to infection; and how this affects the entire community because if you can't afford menstrual products, you can't afford insurance. Finally, she came around after apologizing again to her chief of staff. It was a win but a hard-fought one.

The next meeting was with the head of the Senate Appropriations Committee, but he was in session, so we met with his chief of staff instead. She was lovely. She asked great questions, was very supportive, and said her senator (Democrat, former teacher, male) would also be supportive, and we both left that meeting excited about what might happen.

We also needed to speak to some legislators in the House of Representatives. Initially, both sides of Congress write Michigan's state budget then the executive branch separately. They go into a conference and compare line items, and if the line items are on two proposed budgets, they move the line item to the finalized budget. Even though the Senate budget seemed promising, we needed to be sure we had support on both sides of the aisle.

I was not exactly late but close. I met Maureen's partner, Jeff, at their office, breathless from my run through the bitter wind. I signed our pro bono agreement, and we headed off again. He was tall, and his strides were longer than mine, so I struggled to keep up. We crossed the street and turned toward the Capitol building. The lawn seemed endless, and the wind whipped through me.

We got to the main steps but went through a door I hadn't noticed before. The hush was sudden. We walked with purpose past the guards and turned down the first hallway. I hadn't been in this building since I was in high school, and even then, we weren't downstairs. The detail struck me—the ironwork on the lights, the wooden finials, the beautiful floor. Jeff turned left suddenly, and we took the mirrored elevator to the third floor. He pointed me to the office ahead, said, "Maureen's in there already," and took his leave. I walked through tentatively because I felt like I didn't really belong in this beautiful office. A huge wooden table took up half of the office. Floor-to-ceiling windows highlighted the blustery day outside, and the representative was backlit at her desk, so I couldn't see her face. Maureen motioned me over, and I sat and breathed.

Representative Regina Weiss came over and introduced herself. I half-stood, shook her hand, and told her it was so nice to meet her. We sat, and Maureen asked me to tell a bit about Helping Women Period. I explained we are a nonprofit providing free menstrual products to those experiencing homelessness and low-income disparity. We have been doing this since 2015 and worked with more than eighty schools in Michigan to provide menstrual products to students.

I hoped for a connection. Since Representative Weiss used to be a teacher, surely she would understand the need for menstrual products. We gave her our handout with the data, and Maureen explained our back-of-the-napkin math. She shared it would only take five million dollars to cover the menstrual needs of all the Michigan kids who qualify for free and reduced lunch. Representative Weiss talked about her time teaching in inner-city Detroit and how some schools don't even provide toilet paper because there's so much vandalism. Why, then, would they supply period products? In my head, I think vandalism in bathrooms is indicative of other systemic issues not solved by legislation. I tried to explain we want to give products so kids come to school. But it didn't dawn on me until later to mention it wouldn't be necessary to offer the products in the bathrooms.

We talked a bit about who would decide, know, and help those kids in need. Counselors? Teachers? And how would we implement this program? Did Helping Women Period want to be in charge? Many schools had a McKinney-Vento liaison who knew the unhoused and low-income kids and could help direct the products to those who needed them. The McKinney-Vento Homeless Assistance Act is a federal law that provides rights and services to unhoused children and teens. I reassured Representative Weiss that Helping Women Period was only interested in getting the products to those who could benefit. In fact, if this line item went through, it would cut our distribution numbers in half.

Representative Weiss took notes on her computer the entire time. I hoped she was on our side. She thanked us for coming in, and we thanked her for her time. As we walked back, Maureen seemed confident, and I believed her, but I was still a bit down. I guess I expected more immediate support. But I understood this was the long game. Working with legislators was more difficult this time around. Two years before, when we were working on the tampon tax repeal, legislators had already submitted a bill. We were able to give testimony and bolster what they already knew. This time, we were starting from scratch. I was so used to people immediately seeing the need that it was difficult to process when someone didn't seem to want to help.

I spent a few weeks after the conversation with Representative Weiss alternating between worrying about the proposal and thinking about what we could do differently next year to push it through if it failed this year. Then, in April, I received a text from Maureen. The senators had a proposal for a Helping Women Period pilot project. They would appropriate one million dollars from the school budget to ten school districts across the state for the purchase of pads and tampons for at-risk students to take home during the school year. This was a far cry from the five million dollars I had been hoping for but also much more than I had really expected.

The budget process is interesting in Michigan. The state departments figure out what they need and what they are spending in August. The governor receives their budget requests in October, and agencies convene budget hearings. Following budget hearings, the state legislature receives the governor's proposed budget in February. The legislature can review and adjust the budget before adopting it. Lawmakers strive to adopt the budget by July 1. By law, the governor must sign a final and balanced state budget by October 1, when the new fiscal year begins. Michigan is one of forty states in which the governor can veto specific items, line by line.

We weren't sure if the House would accept the line item. There were some tense moments. On June 20, Maureen texted, "I am at the conference—the line item passed. We did it!" I didn't want to breathe. I didn't really believe her. Political gears move slowly, so I didn't hear anything more about the pilot project until September. The project released money in October. I wanted to know more about who would choose the participating schools, who would administer the grants to those schools, and how the schools would implement the project. I connected with the Department of Education and started talking about the actual implementation because of my personal investment in this project with my organization's name attached to it.

There is so much more that goes into something like this. The approval and appropriation are just the first tiny steps. Then come the big decisions about the grants. What do the schools need to do? What would we *like* them to do? How would we implement this program? Do the kids come to the nurse's office and pick them up, or do we pass them out in homeroom? How can we be respectful of the families' privacy and still get the products to the kids in a timely manner?

One problem with this grant is it just covered the cost of the pads and tampons. It doesn't cover the salaries of those running the program, the bags to hand out the products discretely, or the time to create a survey to find out what students want. The process is fascinating and frustrating in equal measures. I was grateful to be a part of it all and hopeful it would become a permanent change in the way the schools viewed menstrual needs.

I learned so much from this entire experience. Instigation is hard. Sometimes, it feels like you are running up against block after block. Persistence is the key, and being willing to listen to those who oppose your idea or don't understand it helps move the process along. People want to feel heard, so listen to them. After that, you can keep explaining and address their concerns. It is okay to feel frustrated because, after all, discomfort is integral to real change.

CHAPTER 10

PUTTING IT ALL TOGETHER

Instigation doesn't have to be just the tough stuff. It can be really fun to shake up people's expectations in fun ways too.

My husband Craig and my best friend Sherri took me out for breakfast on my birthday. It was spring in Michigan, one of those beautiful days when the sun was shining and the daffodils were blooming. There was still a bit of a chill in the air, but the blue sky and flowers promised warmer days ahead. It was a weekday, and they both took the morning off to celebrate.

After breakfast we decided to go to Old Town—a neighborhood in our town known for cute shops and the beginning of the River Walk, a park that borders the Grand River. My friend Tasma had recently purchased one of those blow-up dinosaur costumes, and we called to invite her along. Unfortunately, she had an appointment, but she dropped the costume off with us. You really don't know freedom until you've been inside one of those outfits. We took turns wearing it—walking down the trail, doing jumping jacks, and laughing. They really look ridiculous exercising! When we walked back toward the main drag, we saw someone leaving the parking lot. Craig was wearing the suit and decided to chase down the car. The driver had to stop before she got to the exit. She rolled down her window, and my heart dropped. I was sure she would yell at us, but she was laughing so hard she had tears on her cheeks. She said seeing the dino in her rearview mirror that had "Objects in mirror are closer than they appear" printed along the bottom was one of the funniest things she'd ever experienced.

We visited a few shops—the bike store (we scared the cat!), a restaurant called Meat, and an office where a friend worked. My favorite experience was at the pet store. Preuss Pets is an amazing place—warm, dim, and humid when you first walk in. To the right are the exotic birds. Straight ahead are the rows and rows of salt and freshwater aquariums. To the left is a small cut-in-half school bus housing many sweet little reptiles. We veered left, went up to the counter, and rang the bell. When the shop assistants arrived, they tried not to laugh and asked how they could help us. Craig did a little dance, shaking the mouth of the costume, and I asked for a million mealworms to tide him over. The owner came over, laughing, and said she was interviewing a prospective employee. Could we walk through the interview so she could see how the employee reacted? She showed us where and told us we could leave through the back door. We sauntered through the interview. I hope the person got the job because they took it in stride. The guy stocking stuff in the back was also pretty chill. "Well, you don't see that every day," he said under his breath as we walked by.

The anonymity of the costume is so freeing. No one can see your face, so while you might feel self-conscious at first, it becomes easier to step out of your comfort zone the longer you are in it. Having a handler is helpful, because that tail gets in the way and your peripheral vision becomes occluded by the costume. We had so much fun that I now own four blow-up dinosaurs, a Pikachu, and a Baymax from *Big Hero 6*. One of the best parts about the whole experience was learning to let go of the discomfort of what I *should* be doing and realizing no one knew who I was. Being able to practice doing things I wouldn't usually do, like dancing on the sidewalk without judgment, made doing things a little uncomfortable outside of the costume much easier.

I believe in you. You don't need a dinosaur costume, but it helps. You can do this. You'll go to your next meeting, class, or workday and look for what needs to happen. You'll be more aware of the issues now. You probably already know some of them. Take a minute and write out a list of things that need to change. Go ahead. I'll wait.

Now, why do those things need to change? You don't like them? Do they hurt a segment of the population? Are they redundant or unnecessary? Your goals need to be do-able. You can't, for example, eliminate capitalism from the store you work for, but you can encourage selling more sustainable products.

If they change, what, if anything, will take their place?

Do others in the group feel similarly? Having at least one coconspirator is so helpful.

As you go out into the world and consider instigation, remember these things.

The instigator has *awareness*. They are paying attention to the big picture. Listening to the group, synthesizing the meat of the issues, and watching the body language of others are integral to the process.

The instigator *asks questions*. These questions help get to the heart of the matter. Like a magnifying glass, the right questions can pull others into the discussion and disrupt the discussion.

Calmness and *an investment in free discourse* are hallmarks of an instigator. It is important to let go of your attachment to a specific outcome. When lasting change happens, it is a collaborative effort and will be better and have more buy-in if it comes from within.

Instigators find *nontraditional solutions*. On those occasions when instigators push forward, it is because traditional solutions aren't working anymore. Take the current teacher shortage, for instance. A panel I heard the other day said we need to solve this problem and increase wages to hire new teachers. That's a valid point. However, the teacher shortage is just a symptom of the systemic issue. Even if they found the money to hire teachers for what they are truly worth, it won't stop the other issues of crumbling schools, poor management, too much parental input, book banning, religious influences, and so on. We really need to dismantle the entire system and come up with a new method.

And finally, an instigator is *quiet, calm,* and *insistent.* In the past few years, we have had a lot of loud public opinions, and sometimes that leads to change, but it is usually divisive. Like a mosquito, the instigator keeps their ideas in the mix, including evidence and experience, until the change comes about.

Quiet leadership is redirecting the conversation and awareness of the power dynamics in the room—a whisper here, a suggestion there. Instigation is both tactical *and* strategic. It sees the details and the big picture and provides both the fuel and the compass. It is not necessarily impulsive. It takes patience and awareness to be a successful instigator. And you can do it!

It is so easy to look at the big things in our world that need to change—wars, poverty, homelessness, apathy—and become depressed. We are bombarded daily, if not hourly, with bad news, decisions made by people in power that affect many but benefit few. War in the Middle East has been a refrain since before I was born. People hold up cardboard signs asking for help, or food, or money, on street corners all over the US. Facebook, Instagram, and X (formerly Twitter) have people spouting off on how horrid, lazy, and unmotivated the other generations are. It is overwhelming. We can choose to let the helplessness swallow us, or we can do something. We need to do what we can. Even the littlest action can create ripples that move across the world. Looking for and sharing the good and the beauty we see every day helps, as does doing small things that help others. This is where instigation comes in.

The museum my grandmother created wouldn't be there if she hadn't asked people for help. Businesses would have failed or not even come to fruition without the Facebook group we started. Thousands of people would have had to choose between food for their kids and pads and tampons for themselves if Amy and I had decided we couldn't host the breakfast when we started Helping Women Period.

One of my favorite stories that helps illustrate this is "The Star Thrower," which is a story in a 1969 book by Loren Eiseley.

It's a gorgeous morning on the beach. The sun comes up, reflecting on the water. The waves are slipping back and forth on the sand, and the air is warm and salty. A terrific storm the night before had finally blown itself out, and the beach is covered with thousands of starfish. A young boy is walking down the beach, picking them up one at a time and throwing them into the water. An old man watches him for a while and finally comes up and asks, "Why are you doing that? It doesn't matter, you won't make a difference to all of them."

The boy stops, looks at the old man, and holds up a starfish. "It makes a difference to this one," the boy says. And he throws it into the water.

He leaves the old man standing there and continues down the beach, throwing starfish in as he walks.

After contemplating for a bit, the old man bends down, picks up a starfish, and throws it back into the water. He slowly works his way back home, tossing starfish as he goes (Eiseley 1972, 160–165)

* * *

I hope you become an instigator and a star thrower. You can make a difference. Just pay attention to the world around you, and when you see something that needs to be done, pick it up and do what you can do. You will be amazed at what happens next.

ACKNOWLEDGMENTS

I wish to thank the myriad of people who helped make this book possible.

My early adopters and supporters, thank you for your belief in me.

Adam Kofinas
Alexa Trifilo
Alicia Biddington
Amy and Michael Stephenson
Andrea Arthur
Andrea Calabrese
Andrea Mobley
Angela Spayde
Anne Spence
Annie Jane Cotten
Beth Harvey
Bob Pratt
Brian Byars
Cammie Jones
Carl B Flotka

Catherine Friedman
Cathy Cooke
Chris Wolfe
Claudia Snyder
Cory McElwee
Cynthia Richartz
Danielle Casavant
Diane Cooke
Dorothy Engelman
Elisabeth Metric
Elizabeth Johnson
Eric Koester
Gabriel Zawadzki
J Meyers
James Aoun
Jane Laycock

Jane Reiter
Jennifer Hanna
Jennifer Schrader
Jessy Gregg
Jill Windahl
Julie Cavanaugh
Julie Hartley
Julie Powers
Julie Steiner
Kathleen Weis
Kathryn Alexander
Katie Krick
Kim Barber
Kristi Hemmer
Laura Atterberg-Sievert
Laura Carpenter Myers
Laura Wallis
Laura Wyble
Laurel Winkel
Laurie Carpenter
Lisa Assenmacher
Lisa Ledl
Lori Gill
Lyah Vansickle
Lynne Ruelaine Stokes
Marcie Timmerman
Margaret Donovan
Mary Prekop
Megan Dowell
Megan Donahue
Melanie McNamara
Melissa Threadgould

Michelle Chambers
Nancy Heerens-Knudson
Nancy Ward
Nick Miron
Nicole Helcher
Nicole McCollum
Pamela Welsh
Paula Brantner
Paula Walz
Regina Carey
Renee Brock
Rina Risper
Roger Breisch
Rose Tantraphol
Ryan Hesseltine
Samantha Jackson
Sara Metz
Sarrah Gani
Shannon Farrar
Sid Beckwith
Stacey Jennings
Starlyn D'Angelo
Stephanie Lewandowski
Stephanie Murray
Sunny Spicer
Susan Denson-Guy
Susie Hyatt
Suzanne Love
Suzie Unruh
Teagan Dixon
Terri Pulice
Valerie Torrey

Veronica Gracia-Wing   Yvonne LeFave
Violet Defiant Livingston   Adam Kofinas
Whitney Spotts

My beta readers: Michael Hood, Kristi Hemmer, and Pamela Welsh.

My cover inspiration creator: Laura Atterberg-Sievert.

My photographer: Sarrah Gani.

The editors, marketing, and cover folks from Manuscripts LLC, especially David Grandouiller, Kristy Elam, Shanna Heath, Sherman Morrison, Frances Chiu, Laura Vaisman-Rivera, Gjorgji Pejkovski, and Bojana Gigovska.

And last, but definitely not least, my family, without whom this book would have never seen the light of day. My kids, Adam and Molly, for making dinner and cleaning up while I was busy writing and working. Liam, for your stalwart belief in me. My dad, Sidney, for his steadfast support my whole life. Finally, my dear husband Craig: You are the best cheerleader, feminist, and hand-holder anyone could ask for. I love you.

APPENDIX

CHAPTER 1

Clear, James. 2018. *Atomic Habits: An Easy & Proven Way to Build Good Habits & Break Bad Ones.* New York: Avery.

Doyle, Glennon. 2020. *Untamed.* New York: The Dial Press.

Rhimes, Shonda. 2015. *Year of Yes: How to Dance It Out, Stand in the Sun, and Be Your Own Person.* New York: Simon & Schuster.

Hemmer, Kristi. 2021. *Quit Being So Good: Stories of an Unapologetic Woman.* Minneapolis: Wise Ink Creative Publishing.

CHAPTER 2

Edwards, Betty. 1989. *Drawing on the Right Side of the Brain.* Los Angeles: Tarcher.

Kay, Katty and Claire Shipman. 2023. *The Power Code: More Joy. Less Ego. Maximum Impact for Women (and Everyone).* New York: Harper Business.

Vredeveld, Peter. 2024. "The Buddha's Philosophy of Non-attachment and the Middle Way." *Original Buddhas* (blog). February 19, 2024. https://www.originalbuddhas.com/

blog/the-buddhas-philosophy-of-non-attachment-and-the-
middle-way.

Williamson, Marianne. 2007. *A Return to Love: Reflections on the Principles of a Course in Miracles.* New York: HarperCollins. E-book format.

CHAPTER 3

Hoose, Phillip. 2009. *Claudette Colvin: Twice Toward Justice.* New York: Melanie Kroupa Books. E-book format.

Neary, Lynn. 1992. "On the Possibility of Arrest" and "Main Reason for Keeping Her Seat" (radio interview) available within "Civil Rights Icon Rosa Parks Dies." *News* (blog), *National Public Radio.* October 25, 2005. https://www.npr.org/2005/10/25/4973548/civil-rights-icon-rosa-parks-dies.

Parks, Rosa with Jim Haskins. 1999. *Rosa Parks: My Story.* London: Puffin Books.

Theoharis, Jeanne. 2013. *The Rebellious Life of Mrs. Rosa Parks.* Boston: Beacon Press. E-book format.

CHAPTER 5

Flint and Genesee Literacy Network. 2018. "Literacy in Flint and Genesee County." Accessed April 20, 2024. https://flintliteracynetwork.org/wp-content/uploads/2018/03/Literacy-Fact-Sheet.pdf.

House, Kelly. 2023. "Michigan Judge Approves $626 Million Flint Water Crisis Settlement." Bridge Michigan. March 21, 2023. https://www.bridgemi.com/michigan-environment-watch/michigan-judge-approves-626-million-flint-water-crisis-settlement.

Parks, Dr. Jeffrey and Anurag Mantha. 2015. "Lead Testing Results for Water Sampled by Residents." Flint Water Study. Accessed April 20, 2024. https://flintwaterstudy.org/information-for-flint-residents/results-for-citizen-testing-for-lead-300-kits.

Pennington, Donna Secor. 2017. *When Things Went Wrong with the Water: A Public Health Catastrophe.* Presentation at The Flint Water Crisis: Systemic Racism through the Lens of Flint, Report of the Michigan Civil Rights Commission. February 17, 2017. https://wmich.edu/sites/default/files/attachments/u98/2017/When%20Things%20Went%20Wrong%20with%20the%20Water%20CDI%202017.pdf.

US Census Bureau. "Quick Facts Flint City, Michigan." Persons in Poverty. Accessed April 20, 2024. https://www.census.gov/quickfacts/fact/table/flintcitymichigan.

CHAPTER 6

Glasser, William. 1965. *Reality Therapy: A New Approach to Psychiatry.* New York: Harper Perennial.

CHAPTER 8

CARES Act. 2020. Public Law No: 116-136 March 27, 2020. https://www.congress.gov/bill/116th-congress/house-bill/748.

MCL-Section 205.54g. 1933. Act 167 of 1933. General Sales Tax Act (Excerpt). https://www.legislature.mi.gov/Laws/MCL?objectName=mcl-205-54g.

Skubick, Tim. 2012. "Michigan Rep. Censored for Use of 'V-Word.'" *CBS News.* June 14, 2012. Accessed April 21, 2024. https://www.cbsnews.com/detroit/news/michigan-rep-censored-for-use-of-v-word/.

CHAPTER 9

Alliance for Period Supplies. 2021. "Michigan State Fact Sheet on Period Poverty." AllianceforPeriodSupplies.org. Accessed March 15, 2024. https://allianceforperiodsupplies.org/wp-content/uploads/2022/05/Michigan.pdf.

MCL-Section 380.1561. 1976. Act 451 of 1976, The Revised School Code. https://legislature.mi.gov/Laws/MCL?objectName=mcl-380-1561.

CHAPTER 10
Eiseley, Loren. 1972. "The Star Thrower" in *The Unexpected Universe.* Boston: Mariner Books.